# MAKING SENSE
## OF
# MARKETING

## Graham Robinson

Formerly Director of the Wigan Management Centre

Open
B/TEC
MACMILLAN

First published 1986 by
MACMILLAN EDUCATION LTD
Houndmills, Basingstoke, Hampshire RG21 2XS
and London
Companies and representatives
throughout the world

ISBN 0–333–42826–9

Printed in Hong Kong

10   9   8   7   6   5
00  99  98  97  96  95  94  93  92  91

The case studies in this book are based on research reports by Richard Maude, and interviews by Ian Rosenbloom for the YTV series *The Marketing Mix*. The author and publishers would like to acknowledge the help given by the following in producing the case studies:

Mike Jolly, Marketing Manager, Madame Tussaud's
John Samuels, Managing Director, British Market Research Bureau
Mary Goodyear, Market Behaviour Ltd
Bob Tyrrell, Director of Social Forecasting, Henley Centre for Forecasting
Alan Benjamin, Director of Communications, CAP Group
Aubrey Wilson
Bradford Economic Development Unit
Ross Marks, Managing Director, Ross Electronics
Nick White, Managing Director, Lune Metal Spinning Company
Tip Top
Cadbury's
Creenagh Lodge, consultant, Craton, Lodge & Knight
Roy Hall Cash & Carry
David Stewart, Conran Design Associates
Allinsons
Ivor Warburton, Assistant General Manager, British Rail London Midland Region
David Jones, Managing Director, Grattan
Robert Wilson, Director, British Wool Marketing Board
National Breakdown
Heuga
Matt McBride, Marketing Director, Heinz
Phil Robson, Taylor Hitec
More O'Ferrall
Richard Gibb, Product Group Manager, Rowntree Mackintosh
General Motors
Jim Birrell, General Manager, Halifax Building Society
Lever Bros
JVC
The National Museum of Photography
Yale Security Services Ltd
*Modern Railways* magazine

The author and publishers would also like to thank the following for permission to reproduce photographs and illustrations:

Automobile Association: Fig. 23
Cadbury's: Fig. 14
Roy Hall Cash and Carry: Fig. 16
Heinz: Fig. 26
Lever Bros: Fig. 25
Madame Tussaud's: Figs 4, 5 and 6
Next: Fig. 9
The Post Office: Fig. 22
PRCA: Figs 19 and 20
Rowntree Mackintosh: Fig. 24
The Stock Exchange: Fig. 8
Tip Top Stores Ltd: Figs 12 and 13

# CONTENTS

Since this workbook was first published in 1986 the recommended text accompanying it has been withdrawn by the publishers. The chart below shows five alternative textbooks which could be used instead, with the new Supplementary Reading references for each chapter of the workbook. Full details of each alternative textbook are given below.

| Workbook Chapter | WILMHURST *Fundamentals of Marketing* | FOSTER *Mastering Marketing* | WILLS *Maximising Marketing Effectiveness* | CANNON *Basic Marketing Principles* | MORDEN *Elements of Marketing* |
|---|---|---|---|---|---|
| | Chapter | Chapter | Chapter | Chapter | Chapter |
| Thinking Marketing | 1, 9 | 1 – 3 | 1 – 6, 25 – 28 | 1 – 4 | 1 – 3, |
| Marketing Through Research | 2, 11, 12 | 4, 6 | 7 – 11 | 5 – 8, 13 | 4 – 6 |
| Product Decisions | 4, 5 | 5.1 – 5.5 | 12 – 14 | 10, 11 14, 15 22, 23 | 19 – 21 |
| Place Decisions | 7 | 8 | 15 – 17 | 9, 17, 18 | 25 – 29 |
| Promotion Decisions | 8, 13 | 7 | 21 – 24 | 19 – 21 | 30 – 37 |
| Pricing Decisions | 6 | 5.6 – 5.8 | 18 – 20 | 16 | 22 – 24 |
| Over to You | 10 | 9 | 29 – 32 | 24 | 43 – 46 |

Alternative textbooks to accompany the workbook *Making Sense of Marketing*.

| Author | Title | Publisher |
|---|---|---|
| WILMHURST John | *Fundamentals of Marketing* | (Heinemann) 2nd Edition 1984 |
| FOSTER Douglas | *Mastering Marketing* | (Macmillan) 2nd Edition 1988 |
| WILLS G, KENNEDY SH, CHEESE J, RUSHTON A | *Maximising Marketing Effectiveness* | (MCB University Press) 8th Edition 1986 |
| CANNON Tom | *Basic Marketing Principles and Practice* | (Holt, Rinehart and Winston) 2nd Edition 1986 |
| MORDEN Anthony R | *Elements of Marketing* | (DP Publications Ltd) 1987 |

# PREFACE

*The Marketing Mix* television series came about because after years of making programmes about business and industry, I despaired at people saying 'We're bad at marketing in Britain'.

Like many people, I thought marketing was something to do with advertising or promotion, or people with clipboards.

Marketing is a philosophy of business based on a simple idea – NO CUSTOMERS, NO BUSINESS.

I am extremely grateful to the businesses, large and small, who have given me the opportunity to show the discipline, practice and fun of marketing in a major Channel 4 series.

Marketing *is* fun, and I hope that by watching the programme, in conjunction with this Workbook, you too will be Making Sense of Marketing.

Iam Rosenbloom
Producer/Director
Yorkshire Television Ltd

# INTRODUCTION

This Workbook is designed to complement the YTV/Channel 4 series **The Marketing Mix.** Its aims to give you an overview of marketing. The Workbook and the television series are designed as an integrated **introductory pack**. If you wish to pursue any of the topics within the package you are recommended to use the **Supplementary Text**, the book *Mastering Marketing,* second edition (Douglas Foster) published in 1984 by Macmillan Education.

The Workbook has seven chapters and each chapter has a short section introducing you to basic marketing theory. This is followed by discussion of the relevant case studies included in the television series.

As you study the text and view the television programmes relating to each chapter, you will be asked to undertake some Activities, which have been designed to help you apply your Marketing knowledge in your real-life situation. In some instances these Activities are relevant to all readers of the Workbook. In others it will be best if you select the most useful.

The Supplementary Text is referred to within the Workbook by chapter. Each chapter in the Supplementary Text contains Assignments which are not compulsory, but which will further extend and reinforce your learning.

## BTEC Continuing Education Award

If you wish your learning to be recognised by the award of a BTEC Certificate of Achievement you will need to use all three elements of THE MARKETING MIX package:

- the television programmes
- this BTEC Open Learning Workbook
- the Supplementary Text

To register with BTEC as a Continuing Education Award student you should contact your Regional Management Centre or local College of Further/Higher Education. Alternatively you may contact:

The Business and Technician Education Council
Central House
Upper Woburn Place
LONDON WC1H 0HH
Tel: 01-388 3288

**You may study at a distance** or as a member of a class, a Business Club or with colleagues. The options are wide open. (This is one of the reasons why it is called an 'open learning' Workbook.) However, in order to receive a Certificate of Achievement you must complete a number of Assignments which will be sent to you and assessed by an established BTEC college or other suitable provider. Successful completion of these practical assignments will lead to the award of a Certificate of Achievement. There will be no formal examination.

## Symbols

Throughout this Workbook you will meet various symbols to help you work through the material.

 Supplementary Reading

 TV programme or video. The figure inside the screen refers to the number of the TV programme in which each case study appears.

You will also see that each Activity is accompanied by a symbol.

 denotes a *reflective activity*, in which you are asked to think for a few minutes about a particular subject, to focus on or reinforce what you have just been reading, and perhaps jot down some notes, before going on to the next piece of work.

 denotes an activity for which a specific *written answer* is required.

# CHAPTER 1

# THINK MARKETING

**M**arketing is concerned with getting the right product to the right customer at the right price. It is not just a fancy word for 'selling'. It is not synonymous with 'advertising' or 'sales promotion': nor is it merely a data-collecting, number-processing and planning activity.

Marketing is more than a set of techniques and it is not just the prerogative of business managers and others who have the word 'marketing' in their job titles. Whilst functional specialists do exist to fulfil important marketing roles, there are many more people who make significant contributions (often unknowingly) to the effectiveness of their organisations' marketing performance.

## 1.1 A Philosophy of Business

Marketing is a philosophy of business which puts the customers and potential customers at the centre of business strategy. And it is the umbrella title given to those operational activities whose aims are to:

- identify customer and potential-customer needs
- determine an optimum product strategy
- ensure the effective distribution of the products
- inform customers of, and persuade them to buy, the products
- determine the prices at which they should be sold

There are many definitions of Marketing, some of which are given in Fig. 1.

Everyone in an organisation should be encouraged to 'think marketing' — to remember that in the long run customers keep a business in business.

Think about a product that you have purchased recently. Which aspect of the manufacturer's/supplier's behaviour demonstrated marketing orientation?

Which aspects of behaviour demonstrated product orientation?

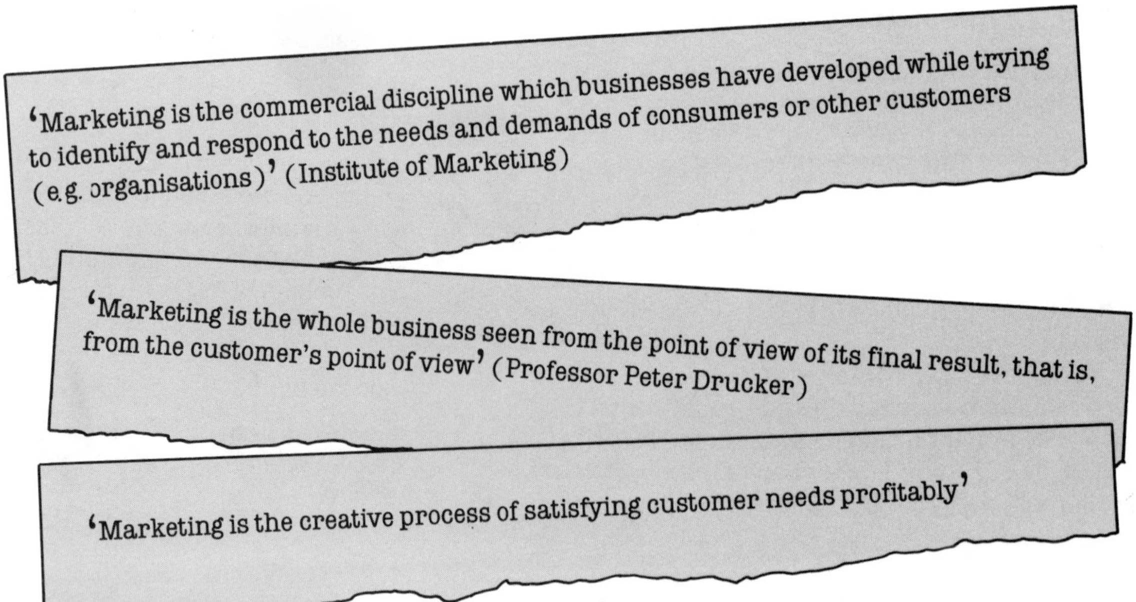

**ACTIVITY 1**

>←

'Marketing is the commercial discipline which businesses have developed while trying to identify and respond to the needs and demands of consumers or other customers (e.g. organisations)' (Institute of Marketing)

'Marketing is the whole business seen from the point of view of its final result, that is, from the customer's point of view' (Professor Peter Drucker)

'Marketing is the creative process of satisfying customer needs profitably'

Fig. 1 There are many definitions of Marketing . . .

**ACTIVITY 2**

Think carefully about your needs as a consumer when you buy food from:

a a fast-food takeaway shop
b a McDonald fast-food café
c a high class restaurant

Now consider the implications for the marketing policy of each of these organisations (e.g. product/environment, promotion and price implications).

## 1.2 A Management Function

It is vital for an organisation to be primarily concerned with the needs and wants of its customers. The most marketing-orientated organisations have employees at all levels and in all sorts of job who 'think marketing'. However, in most organisations it is also essential to employ specialists whose tasks are to ensure that the business is constantly in tune with its markets; that it is constantly matching customer needs to business resources.

The type and size of business will determine the most appropriate organisation and staffing for effective marketing. In a small business the marketing management function may not be evidenced by a post designated 'Marketing Manager' (or similar title).

In many small businesses the owner/manager is indeed the marketing manager (as well as the finance manager, personnel manager etc.). This makes the marketing management role here no less important than that of a full-time marketing manager in a large corporation. Indeed, if a manager spends only part of the time making vital marketing decisions it is essential that these are made in as professional a way as possible.

A larger business may find it necessary to have a number of marketing specialists,

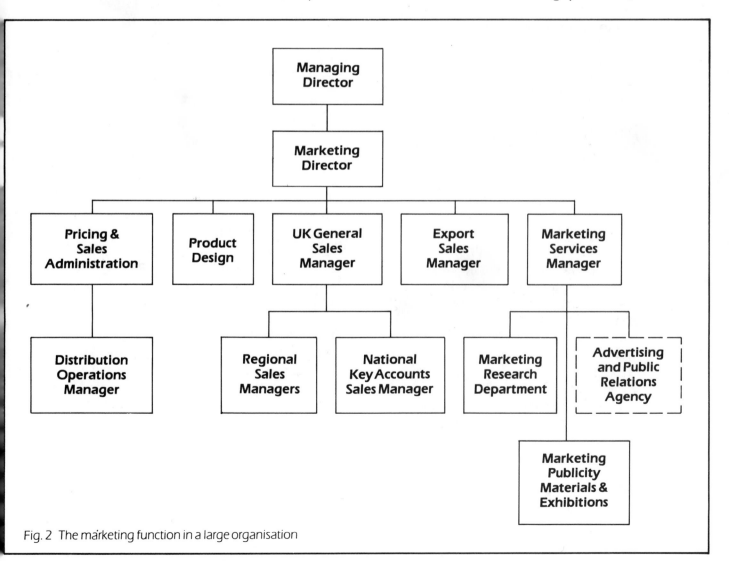

Fig. 2 The marketing function in a large organisation

each responsible for designated marketing operations such as personal selling, advertising and sales literature and distribution (Fig. 2). Many businesses also find it necessary to employ external marketing specialists such as advertising agencies, public relations consultants and market research organisations.

**ACTIVITY 3** Identify the main marketing roles in your organisation (remember that titles may be totally irrelevant to the roles). Is the structure of the organisation conducive to a marketing orientated corporate policy?

**ACTIVITY 4** List the major external opportunities facing your organisation during the next five years.

**ACTIVITY 5** List the potential threats facing your organisation.

## 1.3 Marketing Orientation

The degree to which a company is genuinely marketing orientated cannot be assessed simply by reference to its organisation structure and job titles. Some large companies show all the trappings — large advertising budgets, national and international sales forces, products with a well-known name — and yet are remarkably insensitive to customer needs. Household name companies sometimes crash in the marketplace because they have become too **production-orientated.** They have become short-sighted in marketing terms; they are more interested in selling today's products and facilities than in creating new products to meet the changing patterns of customer needs. An unshakeable conviction that their products are the best in the world, and that people cannot manage without them, can lead to their defeat by companies they have not previously considered to be competitors — companies who, perhaps, are not even perceived to be in the same industry. Many engineering companies have lost out in this way to plastics' manufacturers. And textiles products have been beaten in some markets by paper-based products (e.g. babies' nappies) and plastics.

A marketing orientated business regards external market opportunities — and threats — as importantly as the internal opportunities represented by investment in capital and manpower resources.

## 1.4 The Relevance of Marketing

Manufacturing, retail and service organisations are all featured in **The Marketing Mix** television series of 10 programmes. Programme One poses the questions:

- Could you market baked beans?
- Could you market British Rail?
- Could you market chocolate?
- Could you market software?
- Could you market Madame Tussaud's?

Each chapter of this Workbook includes summaries of the real-life case studies featured in the TV series. They demonstrate the fact that marketing thinking is applicable to organisations in all sectors and of all sizes. The principles of marketing can even be applied to great effect in non-profit organisations: in charities, public service organisations, sports clubs etc.

If you are to 'think marketing' — whether you are the manager of a very small business, the marketing director of a large corporation or the social secretary of a cricket club — you must have a clear view of:

- what your customers need
- what they want
- what it is that causes them to buy
- what the product is to the customer (as distinct from the company's view of the product)

# CASE STUDY 1
# Madame Tussaud's

## THE CHALLENGE

'Could you market Madame Tussaud's?' asked a job advertisment in 1982. Madame Tussaud's, one of the most successful of London's tourist attractions, had begun to experience a decline in admissions from well over 2 million per annum in the 1970s to about 1.8 million in 1981/2 (Fig. 3). At that stage the company decided to adopt a more aggressive marketing policy. They decided to appoint a professional marketing manager with sound brand management experience in a fast moving consumer goods (**fmcg**) company. As the marketing press at the time commented. 'Madame Tussaud's is looking for a baked bean marketer'. They actually appointed Mike Jolly — an experienced fmcg marketer from Cadbury's.

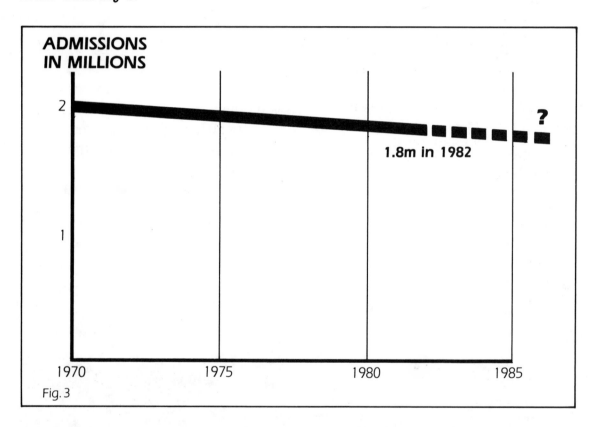

Fig. 3

Jolly's brief was first to arrest the decline in admissions (**sales**) and then to develop a marketing strategy that would enable the company to realise its expansionist ambitions: to develop a new range of attractions (**products**). The company needed to learn how modern marketing disciplines and practices could be harnessed and be made to work for the company.

## MARKETING RESEARCH

We set up quite a lengthy marketing research process [says Mike Jolly]. When I came here I was asked, 'Do you have enough information?' And one of the things I very quickly learnt was that there's an awful lot of statistical information about tourism levels . . . .

So Madame Tussaud's management had access to an impressive bank of already published (**desk research**) marketing information. Jolly took full advantage of this desk research data as he began to develop his understanding of the company's markets.

'...an impressive bank of desk research...'

But the desk research data had its limitations. As a newcomer to the industry Mike Jolly needed to define his **product proposition**. Was the product an exhibition? Was it a museum or gallery? He believed that the word 'museum' had a whole series of negatives — of being fusty, dusty, all behind glass, etc. And the word 'exhibition' was also not ideal. An exhibition shuts; it is usually short-lived. But Madame Tussaud's is permanent and on-going.

The fundamental questions that had to be addressed related to the motivation of Madame Tussaud's customers. So a 'field research' project was undertaken. What were the visitors seeking when they bought a ticket? How did they perceive Madame Tussaud's? What were they buying? Was Madame Tussaud's, in their eyes, a museum — or an art gallery? Who, therefore, were the competitors?

Fig. 4  The product from the customer's point of view

Fig. 5  What was going on between the visitor and the wax figure . . .

Until the company had a firm grasp of the nature of their product from the customer's point of view it could not prepare professional marketing plans. Until he understood what the consumers were really buying, the main benefits experienced by existing customers, the marketing manager could not ensure the maximum effectiveness of his investment in promotional activities: 'I needed to find out more about the sheer process by which visitors enjoy a visit to a wax exhibiton.'

The company's researchers spoke to visitors before and after visiting. Both UK and overseas visitors were interviewed as interviewers attempted to get under the customer's skins. The results were intriguing:

> 'We discovered that the wax figures and all the other special effects that go with some of the wax figures largely are the means to an end because the satisfaction that the visitor derives is largely internal . . . . The enjoyment was not so much the intrinsic art of the wax figure — it was actually what was going on between the visitor and the wax figure; the role of fantasising about the meeting of such a figure, what it would be like, what one would say if one ever met such a figure, what those figures meant to people. And because it is in three dimensions that reality worked for visitors; they thoroughly enjoyed that. They did not find it easy to articulate that enjoyment.'

## PRODUCT DEVELOPMENT

Of what value was this research exercise to the management? It caused the company to think about the product in a different way. To 'think marketing' was to think differently! The traditional tableaux displays, established over 200 years ago, were augmented by more informal, much more relaxed, much more modern displays. Special effects and other sophisticated techniques were developed dramatically to enhance and further stimulate the interaction between the visitor and the exhibit. More opportunities were created for visitors to get close to the wax figures — to relate to them.

## PROMOTIONAL ACTIVITIES

The really big problem was how to communicate to potential customers the benefits of visiting Madame Tussaud's. Museums and many art galleries offered free admission. Why should a visitor pay an economic admission fee for Madame Tussaud's? How could the company promote its unique selling proposition (**usp**)?

Madame Tussaud's had always spent money on publicity. What was new in 1982/3? The company was now adopting a systematic approach to its marketing activities. It had undertaken a critical self-appraisal — a **position audit**. It had acquired new facts about its customers and potential customers. It had begun to **market through research** – to base its marketing plans on sound marketing information. The new approach to promoting the company seeks to brand the product and to develop a distinctive corporate identity: an identity that distinguishes the business from competitors for the tourist £; an identity that is uniquely associated with the Madame Tussaud's experience. A new logo (Fig. 6) was designed and replaced the diffuse range of symbols and words previously used.

The consumer research had revealed that the word 'waxworks' was a very negative term. But it was the only one that the public tended to cling to because there was no other word the public could use. The company has therefore attempted to link the familiar with their new lively advertising themes in the slogan:

Fig. 6

The company had to increase its investment in marketing communications. It had to persuade non-customers of the special Madame Tussaud's proposition. They chose to use a mix of television and print media advertising. A light-hearted, humorous approach was adopted in the television advertisements. The informality, the atmosphere, the humour and the enjoyment were projected strongly.

Television advertising proved very effective in recruiting customers in the London area. To reach the very important overseas market segments the company uses posters around London, again emphasising the fun and enjoyment benefits; and the topicality of the show. The humble leaflet also plays an extremely important role in the Tussaud's promotional tactics. The company claims to be the largest distributor of leaflets in the London hotels. These leaflets reach both domestic and overseas customers. The traditional Tussaud leaflets comprised a series of rectangular photographs of individual portraits. The new, marketing-led leaflets use specifically commissioned photographs that reflect the fact that visitors come to the exhibition to enjoy themselves — pictures of people interacting with wax figures and soaking up the atmosphere.

Madame Tussaud's makes full use of professional public relations techniques. Unlike many manufacturing businesses there is no shortage of stories of real interest to the press, not only in the UK but around the world. It therefore seeks to manage its press relations activities very carefully. One of the problems with PR is that the press photography often does not do justice to a wax figure. The marketing manager therefore goes to considerable trouble to guide the most relevant press people in their photographing and reporting of, for instance, the up-dating of new figures — of national luminaries. He constantly seeks to dovetail the PR activities with the other elements of the company's promotional plans.

## PRICING THE PRODUCT

Getting the product right and communicating an exciting and appealing image to potential customers are necessary prerequisites for the generation of profitable sales. But the actual sale involves a financial transaction. A price must be placed upon the product. How should Madame Tussaud's establish their prices? To many people a price is a matter for calculation. It is directly related to costs (**cost-plus pricing**). But the professional marketer regards pricing as a marketing problem.

The majority of the costs of running Madame Tussaud's are **fixed costs** — they do not vary as the number of customers varies. The key to the profitability of the business is, therefore, the volume of paying visitors. 'Pricing is as much to do with value for money as it is to do with cost or with absolute price levels,' says Mike Jolly. 'There is a general level of expenditure for the family-day-out market, in which we very much see ourselves; that we should not step outside.'

Since adopting their new marketing policy the company has developed greater sophistication in its pricing. Using the newly gained detailed understanding of their customers they have grouped them into homogeneous market segments and priced according to the specific needs of each segment. For example there are now different prices for:

an adult and a child
adults in groups
senior citizens
families of two adults plus two children
summer season visitors
winter season visitors
visitors before 10 a.m.
visitors after 4 p.m.

## PROFIT FROM MARKETING

The company is managing its price structure as a key element of The Marketing Mix. It is investing in product and environmental development. It has increased its investment in promotional activity. And it has been creative in developing a pricing strategy that is compatible with its new corporate image. To what effect? The company has reversed the falling trend in admissions. It has already increased its number of customers from 1.8 million to 2.25 million per year. 'Thinking marketing' has meant a return to long-term business prosperity for Madame Tussaud's.

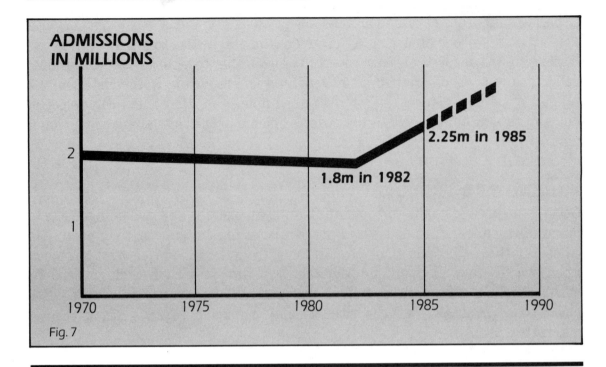

ADMISSIONS
IN MILLIONS

2.25m in 1985

1.8m in 1982

2

1

1970     1975     1980     1985     1990

Fig. 7

**ACTIVITY 6**

Identify two or three distinct market segments served by your organisation (refer to the Madame Tussaud's market segmentation for pricing purposes) and consider how the promotional strategy for each should differ in order to cater for their special needs.

**ACTIVITY 7**

You are an experienced joiner. You have been made redundant and are considering setting up in business on your own. Combining your savings and redundancy money you have approximately £15,000 of initial capital. Identify three or four markets you could investigate in which you could use your knowledge and skills. Then for each of these business opportunities determine what market information you will require in order to assess the viability of each opportunity.

a                                    c

b                                    d

Chapters 1, 2, 3

## CHAPTER 2

# MARKETING THROUGH RESEARCH

## 2.1 Marketing Plans

Marketing is a process of exchange in which buyers and sellers are brought together through transactions in the market place.

Fig. 8  '. . . transactions in the marketplace . . .'

Products should be developed (or purchased for resale) to meet known **customer needs**. The Madame Tussaud's case study demonstrated how a professional marketer brings a **systematic approach to the marketing process**. This process starts with the preparation of a **marketing plan**.

A marketing plan requires decisions to be taken under four main headings. Decisions on:

**P**roducts
**P**lace
**P**romotion
**P**rice  }  The 4 **P**s

A professionally prepared marketing plan is based upon facts and objective market analysis. To be successful without unnecessary risk the plan should be prepared against a background of up-to-date market intelligence data.

## 2.2 Types of Research

**Desk research**, using existing internal and external data, is the first source of market intelligence information. **Field research** techniques are used to acquire data which does not exist in an already published form. The techniques of field research include both large-scale attitude surveys and small-scale depth interview projects.

## 2.3 Managing the 4 Ps

Marketing research processes seek to provide data which assist the marketer to make rational decisions in the planning and control of marketing operations: **the key Marketing Mix decisions**. The effective management of the 4 Ps is the task of the marketing manager (by whatever title). The marketing function must acquire sufficient understanding of customer needs to enable it to generate the optimum mix of products, in the right place, at the right time, with the right level of promotion and at the optimum price. The professional marketer can be said to **market through research**.

This does not mean that all businesses need to spend huge sums on formal marketing research projects. The Industrial Marketing Research Association (IMRA) defines marketing research as:

The systematic, objective and exhaustive search for and study of facts relevant to any problem in the field of marketing.

So marketing research is not the exclusive domain of the clipboard-carrying high street interviewer.

## 2.4  Desk Research

Considerable quantities of valuable marketing information exist inside most businesses. For example records of:

- client organisations
- the activities of sales personnel
- sales, analysed by
  - customer type
  - order size
  - geographical spread
  - season
- records of complaints
- records of enquiries

In the Madame Tussaud's case study we noted that the new marketing manager made full use of all desk research sources of marketing information. In addition to the company's own in-house data he used the wealth of published data on the tourism industry. Only when these desk sources could not provide the required answers did he use field research methods — questioning customers and potential customers to discover unpublished information.

In most markets there are many external desk sources — official and non-official — of marketing information: government reports, official statistics, trade associations, chambers of commerce, NEDO (National Economic Development Office) publications, Monopolies Commission reports, etc. Two useful official publications are:

**Guide to Official Statistics**
**Regional Statistics**

Both are published by and available from Her Majesty's Stationery Office and through good-quality bookshops. In addition, advice on the availability of statistical data relating to many markets and products can be obtained from:

The Central Statistical Office (CSO)
Great George Street
London SW1

The Business Statistics Office
Cardiff Road
Newport
Gwent

The CSO publishes annually a booklet entitled *Government Statistics: A Brief Guide to Sources* which contains the names and telephone numbers of the main Ministries and Departments responsible for particular economic data.

List the sources of information that already exist inside your organisation which could be used in marketing planning/decisions.

**ACTIVITY**
**8**

Non-official external sources of desk research are also in plentiful supply in many markets. Two useful guides are:

*Sources of UK Marketing Information* by Elizabeth Tupper and Gordon Wills (Benn, 1975)
*Principal Sources of Marketing Information* by Christine Hall (Times Newspapers)

The serious national press, trade and technical journals are all rich sources of desk research data. These are augmented by the reports and publications of commercial research and consultancy firms (e.g. The Economist Intelligence Unit, Mintel, Extel) and official Yearbooks or Directories.

All of this may seem to be dry and possibly academic to you, as a person in business. But suppose your business is somewhat dependent upon a particular age group. Some knowledge of trends in the birth rate would certainly be of relevance to you. Unless you are in markets catering for children, or the parents of young people, the birth rate gives you many years' notice of a long-term change in total market potential. In some businesses this could have a bearing on capital expenditure and even on marketing plans.

**ACTIVITY 9**

During the 1990s the 25–44 age group will increase as a proportion of the total population. What business opportunities (and threats) is this change likely to bring for your (or any other) business?

After completing this Activity please read the case study on pages 27–33.

## 2.5  Field Research

While desk research is the least expensive type of marketing research activity, it often cannot provide all the answers that arise before the marketing plan can be finalised. It is usually of restricted value when information on attitudes and qualitative data are required. Field research is the process of collecting data for the first time **(primary**

information)** by asking customers or potential customers or by observing their behaviour. There are two main categories of field research — **quantitative** and **qualitative**. The former seeks to answer questions like:

● How many?
● How valuable?
● What share?
● What percentage growth/fall?

Qualitative research seeks to answer the question 'Why' It probes aspects of customer behaviour which are difficult to measure — needs, attitudes, beliefs, opinions, perceptions and prejudices. The Madame Tussaud's case study demonstrates the importance of exploring these dimensions if we are to understand our buyers' behaviour, and if we are to use The Marketing Mix creatively to influence buyer behaviour favourably.

**ACTIVITY 10**

Ask yourself:

a 'Why do people buy from our organisation?' and

b 'Why do people tend to stop buying our products and switch to other suppliers?'

Make some notes on how you could obtain information on these matters.

a

b

The planning and implementing of field research projects is a very specialised business. A business can conduct a survey of all of its existing or potential customers only rarely. Some form of selection, of sampling, must be undertaken — especially if the results are to be statistically significant. If you intend to conduct a field research exercise you are advised to read an appropriate text on marketing research or business statistics such as *Marketing Research* by Sunny Crouch or *Using Statistics in Business 1* by Peter Clark (both published by Pan).

The techniques of random sampling have been devised in a way that gives each possible buyer an equal chance of being included. In order to reduce the cost of sampling without prejudicing the value of a survey a **quota sample** may be used. Such a sample would contain respondents roughly in proportion to your knowledge of these proportions in the total market (e.g. if you know that 30 per cent of the population is between 35 and 54 years then 30 per cent of the sample must fall within this age band).

In many situations small scale surveys, which will not yield statistically significant data, can be very valuable to a marketing manager. For example, a small manufacturer of wooden window frames commissioned an industrial marketing consultant to conduct face-to-face interviews with between 15 and 20 industrial buyers (in the building industry) and specifiers (architects). Seventeen interviews were conducted with influential buyers and specifiers. The interviews typically lasted between 45 and 90 minutes. The researcher's conclusions and recommendations led to changes in product design, sales representation and sales literature.

## 2.6 Continuous Research

Until the late 1960s such market research as was undertaken was usually conducted on an *ad hoc* basis. This type of research is strictly related to specific tasks and problems. However, during the late 1960s and 1970s the market research techniques and systems available to British businesses developed apace. It is now possible for businesses to monitor their marketing environment on a continuous basis. Companies of all sizes can now make use of national marketing intelligence systems relatively economically. The case study section of this chapter includes descriptions of omnibus marketing research opportunities offered by the British Market Research Bureau. Many other omnibus research services are offered by professional marketing consultancy organisations (see *Marketing Research* for further examples).

'. . . each possible buyer has an equal chance of being included . . .'

# CASE STUDY 2
# Marketing Research

**2**

John Samuels, Managing Director of the British Market Research Bureau, was interviewed to discover his views on the nature and role of marketing research. This section draws on this interview to extend and illustrate the theory section of the chapter.

## MARKETING RESEARCH EXPENDITURE IN THE UK

'It doesn't cost much to do market research,' claims John Samuels, 'relative to the cost of producing and advertising products. Less than 0.2 of 1 per cent of the cost of production is typically spent on market research.' This low investment in obtaining facts prior to making marketing decisions is surprising bearing in mind that many marketing specialists claim that 80 per cent of new products fail.

'Market research didn't really take off in Britain until the advent of commercial television in the late 1950s. It had a second great upturn in the 1960s — with the advent of the computer. And while we had setbacks in the oil price recession of the 1970s we have weathered the recent recession very well indeed. There was no downturn in market research expenditure during that period. I estimate the market research industry's sales turnover at around £200 million per annum. And there are about 45,000 people working in market research.'

So marketing research is becoming increasingly recognised as an essential part of 'thinking marketing' — the basis of sound Marketing Mix decisions.

## *AD HOC* VERSUS CONTINUOUS RESEARCH

When a marketer has a particular problem to solve or a one-off project to implement he may commission an **ad hoc** research survey; a one-off piece of research to solve a one-off problem. For instance a brand manager may wish to check the likely reactions of consumers to the reduction in the range of colours from, say, five to three. This would call for an *ad hoc* research survey.

In contrast **continuous research** is research where the same measurements and research activities are taken continuously, such as the number of tubes of toothpaste sold through shops in Britain every week, and so on.

One of the best known continuous research organisations in the United Kingdom is A C Neilson & Co Ltd, Oxford. The Neilson company plots the flow of goods through shops every week. Neilson interviewers go to every shop in their panel. The Neilson field staff are, in effect, auditors of retail stocks. They check stocks and purchases by retailers at regular and frequent intervals. The results of this distribution audit give subscribers to the Neilson service a regular view of such factors as:

1  market size, and the trends within it
2  market shares, and the trends observed
3  retail stock levels
4  a manufacturer's market penetration

The Heinz marketing managers might use Neilson data to answer the questions:

'Are we selling more or as much product as, say, Crosse and Blackwell? Has our performance this month improved or deteriorated since last month? Does our performance vary from one part of the country to another?'

'Another example would be a service that my company runs for the travel industry,' says Samuels. 'We have a regular panel of travel agents who are visited by interviewers once each month. The interviewers check detailed information about the holidays they have sold: whether there's a trend towards bookings for Greece or Yugoslavia, towards using larger or smaller agencies, to book later or earlier, to hire a car or not, etc.'

'We also run the English hotel occupancy survey. This tells us the monthly statistics on the extent to which UK hotel rooms are occupied, whether they are occupied by the British, or people from abroad, how long the average visitor is staying — and so on.'

## THE TARGET GROUP INDEX (TGI)

This special service offered by the British Market Research Bureau is claimed to be the largest single survey in Britain. 24,000 people answer TGI questionnaires each year, spread evenly across almost every day of the year.

'What they are asked to do is literally to tell us about their lives,' says John Samuels. 'We use comprehensive questionnaires which might include, for example, a small section on shampoos — or toilet soap — holidays or banking — television viewing and newspaper reading. We also ask them something about themselves as people — their lifestyles: whether they're the sort of people who prefer to look for bargains or to shop where it's easiest; whether they like to go out a lot — or to stay at home . . .'

The TGI is sold whole or in part to subscribers. Manufacturers frequently subscribe to a partial service whereas advertising agencies often subscribe to the whole service. Its value is that you can analyse retail sales audit data to find out more about the people who buy competitors' (and your own) brands — to find out, for example, which newspapers these people read, and what their television habits are.

## USING CONTINUOUS RESEARCH TO INFLUENCE RETAILERS

Over the last decade there has been an enormous increase in the power of the retailer relative to the manufacturer. Even large manufacturers experience difficulty in selling to some large retail groups. The development of 'own label' (the retailers' own brand names) merchandise is evidence of the switch of bargaining power from manufacturers to retailers.

When a manufacturing company uses continuous research surveys it has access to retailing data on the flow of its goods, and those of its competitors, to the consumers. The manufacturer will be able to see frequent Neilson reports on the percentage of his and his competitors' products being sold through supermarkets, through chains of independent retailers, through corner shops, and so on.

By consulting the TGI reports the manufacturer can find out what sort of people are buying, for example, Daz, and what sort of people are buying Persil. They could discover where they were located, whether they were heavy purchasers, which media they read (or viewed) etc. Armed with all this information a manufacturer could approach a strong retailer with a proposition such as . . .

> 'We aren't as strong in supermarkets as we should be, nor are we as strong as some of our rivals. We have an enormous number of loyal customers; customers who buy regularly and in large quantities. The most popular pack size in the other regions is the magnum — the size that would give you the highest profit margin. Our total market share is increasing by about 15 per cent per annum. Can you afford to miss this profit opportunity?'

## LOW COST FIELD RESEARCH — OMNIBUS SURVEYS

Although the costs of market research are usually small relative to production and marketing costs they can still represent a significant cash outlay; especially for the smaller business. An **omnibus survey** is a research method which offers a very cost effective opportunity to ask a single question, or a small number of questions, of a large sample of people.

'An omnibus survey is exactly what it sounds. It is a vehicle,' says John Samuels, 'for carrying many questions. It is directed to a particular destination (research audience) and each question shares in the total cost of using the vehicle.'

If you want to reach a large sample with very few questions an omnibus survey is often ideal. Such research services are available for a few hundred pounds from specialist research houses.

# CASE STUDY 3
# Qualitative Research

In the view of Mary Goodyear of Market Behavoir Ltd:

> 'The essential difference between qualitative and quantitative research is concerned with sample size and interview/questionnaire structure. Qualitative research is much more concerned with small research samples. And the interviewees are frequently interviewed in groups ('group discussions'). Qualitative research normally does not have a statistical reliability because of the sample size.'

The size of the sample is not the only reason for the lack of statistical reliability of qualitative surveys. In a qualitative study the interviewer does not control the interview or group discussion.

A qualitative survey interview or discussion group is an **interactive process**. The interviewee can lead the interview in all directions. He or she can often decide the whole arena of discussion and even the momentum of the interview. The example given below will illustrate this.

Before conducting a qualitative research project into processed cheese, a researcher does his/her homework to refine the brief, and acquires as much information as possible about the dairy industry and the marketing of dairy products. All available desk research is read and analysed:

- What are the leading brands?
- What are the market shares?
- Who uses which products?
- What trends exist?
- What are the main substitutes?

Having examined the desk research data the **research objectives** are finalised. Qualitative research is usually undertaken by external research consultants, many of whom are trained in psychology.

A discussion group normally has 4–9 members. More than this will reduce the chance of full participation by all group members.

The interviewers/moderators are usually given a quota of interviewees to recruit, reflecting the composition of the total market. Maybe you want to talk to housewives aged between 25 and 35 years, all of whom bought processed cheese at least twice during the past month. You may also wish to specify their socio-economic grouping and their geographical background.

Members of research discussion groups are often given some type of financial or other incentive. (Typically £5 per person, but sometimes as much as £50 if the interviewee is more difficult to get, especially if inconvenient location or travel are involved.)

In leading the group the 'moderator' (researcher) will need to put the group fully at ease, usually using innocuous questions which are not directly related to the survey objectives, such as

Where do you normally do your grocery shopping?

Is it locally?

What ranges of brands are available?

Do you tend to shop in the same retail outlets from week to week?

Once the group is warmed up specific questions on dairy products are introduced and explored.

It is common for research discussion groups to be audio-recorded. Sometimes they are video-recorded as well.

---

## CASE STUDY 4

# The Henley Centre for Forecasting

Marketing in the late 1980s and the 1990s will bring new challenges to British companies. A sound marketing plan attempts to match business strengths to market opportunities in a manner that satisfies genuine market needs.

All businesses face different combinations of strengths, weaknesses, opportunities and threats. However, trends do exist, and this section aims to present a number of them. It draws heavily upon the work of Bob Tyrrell of the Henley Centre for Forecasting. Whenever a quotation is printed in this case study it is attributable to Bob Tyrrell. However, the author accepts full responsibility for the development of these valuable commentaries within the text.

### SOME SOCIO-ECONOMIC FACTORS

The purchasing of consumer goods is obviously affected by a range of economic factors:

- the general buoyancy of the economy
- unemployment
- levels of taxation
- the distribution of income

Over the past decade there has been a very significant redistribution of income in the UK:

> 'From 1976 to 1981 the distribution of income widened and more than wiped out the trends towards equality that we saw from the post-war period up to 1976. By 1984 that change in the distribution pattern had reached astronomical proportions.
>
> If you look at the share of total income of the top 20 per cent of households, by 1984 we reckon their share of the consumers' cake had increased by about £7 billion. Had they only maintained the share that they had in 1976, today they would be about £7 billion worse off than is the case.'

This has several implications for the marketer.

## POSITIONING ON THE PRICE SPECTRUM

It means that the prosperity of different products is changing according to where they are positioned in the market's range of prices; according to whether or not they are priced low or they enjoy a premium price. In the retail business the success of Marks and Spencer is legendary. Their reputation for success based upon the retailing of high quality products is such that others have followed in other markets. In food Sainsburys, Asda and Tesco have moved up to the premium end of the mass-production markets. But this upward trend on the retail scene has not prevented Kwiksave from developing a down-market fast-moving consumer goods business on the same high streets. Markets are tending to polarise, reflecting the development of the 'two nations' (the poor and the well-off) phenomenon. It is increasingly common to find considerable marketing activity at each end of the pricing spectrum, with very little happening in the mid-price range.

So the dramatic change in distribution of income is having a fundamental social impact and a corresponding impact upon the consumer marketing processes.

## DEMOGRAPHIC FACTORS

> 'Britain over the next 10 years will see the end of youth markets — that's guaranteed'

'... the end of youth markets ...'

Simple projection of the birthrate and mortality statistics indicates that between the National Census years of 1981 and 1991 the number of young people between 16 years of age and 24 years of age will decline by about 850,000 — a 12 per cent fall in numbers. So the number of potential buyers in this market segment is falling dramatically. The impact is compounded for the marketer because there is also an economic dimension. The high levels of youth unemployment have reduced the buying power (per head) of young people.

## GROWTH IN 25–44-YEAR-OLDS GROUP

On the positive side there is a growth in what statisticians refer to as the **family formation group**: people in the 25–44 years age band. Between 1981 and 1991 this group will grow by 1.7 million — a growth of about 16 per cent. And unemployment in this segment is in many parts of the country only a quarter of the youth unemployment level. So this is a growing market that has a higher spending power per head than the youth market. The more mature markets will become more valuable than the youth markets. You can see this happening already on the high street. The Levi Strauss organisation (best known for its branded denims 'Levi's') is busily engaged in re-adjusting its consumer image. It is wooing the more mature kind of consumer group through its advertising programme — with not a blue denim in sight! The emergence of retail chains like Next and Principles alongside the boutiques aiming at the youth markets is further evidence of the lucrative 'maturing' markets for clothing.

Fig. 9

## CHANGE IN FAMILY STABILITY AND LIFESTYLES

It is a sad fact of life that there has been a dramatic increase in the divorce rate since the 1960s. In the mid-1960s there was 1 divorce for every 16–17 marriages. This had deteriorated to 1 for every 2.7 marriages by 1984. Is marriage less popular? No, the deterioration arises entirely from the increase in divorces. Marriage has never been more popular. Indeed even people who have had an unsuccessful marriage often try again. In 1984 35 per cent of marriages were second marriages for one or other of the partners.

What does this mean for the marketer? Traditionally we have come to expect a family to be formed by a couple in their early twenties. Children typically follow after a few years. The growth and development of the children has had a fairly predictable impact upon purchasing needs and habits throughout the traditional family life cycle. Some 40 or more years after marriage one of the partners could be expected to die and a new one-person household formed.

With the new **rate of turnover of households** this traditional pattern has been changed significantly. The financial independence of women in this less stable social environment has become much more important. More women now wish to continue working throughout their married lives for many reasons — but the economic imperative is particularly dominant in the 1980s.

The setting up of new homes, by newly-weds or by divorced single people, means an increased demand for new sets of furniture, electrical appliances, carpets and so on. The single-person household sector is larger than it has ever been. In the mid-1960s it represented 11 per cent of the British market. It has now grown to about 25 per cent of all British households. This is a result partly of the falling mortality rate. It is also a reflection of the transient single-person householder — the divorcee.

## LEISURE AND TECHNOLOGY

Much is said about the increase in leisure time and leisure activities. Many businesses are seeking their fortunes in the growing leisure markets. Undoubtedly the public involvement in leisure pursuits is increasing at a fast pace and can be expected to continue. The marketer must dig beneath the superficial appearance, however. In many leisure markets there is a contrast between **time intensity** and **money intensity**. There are some leisure activities where people spend considerable amounts of money and very little time. There are others that require not much money but take up a considerable amount of time. Hiking, and even gardening, fall into this second category. A careful analysis of your target markets is necessary before investing resources behind leisure products and services. Henley Centre for Forecasting's overall analysis indicates that people are increasingly regarding their **homes as leisure centres**. The recent growth trends in leisure markets have not generally been in leisure services. Otherwise would pubs, spectator sports and bingo halls have experienced the market difficulties they have all suffered?

‘People are now doing it themselves and doing it in their homes. . . .’

Videos are strong competitors to cinemas. Home entertaining is competing with pubs. And the kitchen is becoming a mechanised efficient workshop.

'. . . homes as leisure centres . . .'

The demographic trends, the emergence of the 25–44 year-old market, the change in domestic lifestyles, the increasing availability of leisure time and facilities combined with the sophisticated domestic equipment that is now so easily available come together to reinforce the concept of the home as the leisure centre. The growing number of 25–44 year-olds will be increasingly predisposed to spend time and money in and around their homes. This is all good news for manufacturers of consumer durable goods, and maybe for the small local shopkeeper.

## THE 'CELLULAR HOUSEHOLD'

While people are spending more time in their homes, they are not necessarily spending that extra time as a family group. Evidence of this is the duplication of ownership of consumer durables such as televisions and cassette recorders. The new generation of electronic equipment facilitates an individual pattern of activity within a household. The video recorder allows the viewing of two competing broadcasts. It allows a re-scheduling of viewing to meet an individual's needs. The microwave oven-cum-freezer system allows people to eat at different times with minimum inconvenience. All of these, and other, factors point to the increasing independence that may be reflected in their purchasing decisions and attitudes. 'The key idea that we've come up with', says Tyrrell, 'is that of the connoisseur consumer'. People can be expected to regard their consumption activities in a rather more serious, professional fashion.

## CHANGING PATTERN OF INHERITED WEALTH

There will be an increasing number of people inheriting sizeable estates. Large sums of money will come, suddenly, into the hands of people who previously would never have expected this to happen. People from all social groups in their middle age will actually have parents who are dying and leaving them substantial wealth.

The work of the building societies and life assurance companies in the 1950s has been completed as valuable houses are left and life assurance policies mature. So, many people will inherit £20,000 to £60,000; people who have never seen such monies before. They will need the services of specialist financial advisers. Opportunities for financial consultants and banks will continue to grow. More people will buy second homes.

## MARKET GROWTH AREAS IN THE 1990s

'If you look at all the things that we analyse there are some clear pointers for the future. . . .'

### Major doubt over the service sector

People seem to be in their own homes doing their own things quite happily.

'It's not the service economy we're moving into — it's the self-service society.'

The implications of this are that the manufacturing industry should not be 'written off'! The self-service economy will still require the manufacture of products.

'The average kitchen of the twenty-first century is going to be like a factory.'

This is all good news for housebuilders and homeowners; for furniture manufacturers, fabric suppliers and lighting businesses. It is good for the suppliers of all things that relate to people's time and to their homes.

### Rental markets

With the growth of turnover of households there may be a rental market in furniture. The rental market for private properties could also come back into its own in the 1990s.

### Growth in 'mid years' markets
As the youth markets decline the opportunities for development of the 25–44 years markets will flourish.

### The 'connoisseur consumer'
The emergence of the connoisseur consumer implies smaller markets for many more products. It implies the growth in non-branded high-quality products — products which will be purchased by professional informed consumers. Marketing to the consumer will become more like industrial marketing is today.

### The importance of discounted and generic products
The 'two nations' phenomenon suggests that the established bottom end trend of consumer markets — towards discounted products and generic products — will continue. There will probably continue to be plenty of room for the Kwiksave types of operator; for the Tesco of the 1950s philosophy:

'Pile it high and sell it cheap.'

## CASE STUDY 5

# The CAP Group (I)

The company builds information systems — software, not hardware. In 1984 the company believed there was a need to address the real communication needs of developing countries. CAP combined with other companies to develop a high-tech Land Rover equipped with the very latest communications equipment: VHF, satellite discs, fax, telex, slow scan video, data processing, word processing, viewdata etc. This was to be a public relations vehicle for the 'Mobility 84' project in World Communications Year.

When natural disasters occur in developing countries there is usually no information available to their governments. Loss of roads, rivers, telephone lines, etc. makes it necessary to despatch people into the disaster areas for 10 days and more to find out what really is happening. The new Land Rover would make a very valuable contribution in disaster relief under these circumstances.

### MARKET RESEARCH
The CAP product was the software, the programs at the core of the Land Rover's facilities.

Having developed the product it was vital to the company that they discover if there were sufficient customers who had enough money to buy the product. 'It was very important not to rush off into the market and start selling something when we had no idea whether there was a desire for it. We had some information that suggested that there was a desire, but it was a question of priorities as well,' says Alan Benjamin, Director of Communication.

So the company commissioned Aubrey Wilson, an industrial market research consultant, to research the market. Information was required about potential customers and their ability to pay. The survey involved field research in four countries in different parts of the world: an advanced country, a semi-developed country, a developing country and a basic country in which there was very little communication. The project took four months and led to the production of a thick report which gives a careful analysis of the company's prospects for sales of CAP software to various kinds of customers in the different countries.

## MARKETING PROBLEMS

The research report also identifies the problems that would be faced as the company launched into these markets. Each of the markets researched had its own different problems. The outcome was that the company's substantial investment in the market research project led them to **decide not to proceed to market the product** until further more precisely targetted research had been conducted. One or two countries need to be researched a little further to see whether in fact the company could sell in specific situations.

 Chapters 4, 6

# CHAPTER 3

# PRODUCT DECISIONS

Let us remind ourselves of what marketing is . . .

Marketing is the **creative process** of satisyfing **customer needs** profitably.

A marketing oriented organisation seeks to be creative in all aspects of its relationships with its environment. Creativity in marketing should not be restricted to the marketing communications processes. A business needs to identify clearly who its customers are — both the ultimate and the intermediary customers.

We have already seen the variety of marketing research tools available to help in this process (Chapter 2 and Programme 2). You should remember that marketing research is a means to an end. The end product of a useful marketing research exercise should be data that is valuable in the marketing decision-making processes. And perhaps the most fundamental type of marketing research data relates to customers, their needs and perceived needs.

## 3.1 Matching Business Strengths with Market Opportunities

Businesses of all ages and track records need, from time to time, to undertake a critical self appraisal — a position audit whose aim is to identify:

. . . their

# Strengths,
# Weaknesses, and the
# Opportunities and
# Threats . . .

. . . they face in the marketplace

A soundly based product strategy will seek to reconcile these **SWOT** elements within the context of the overall aims and policy of the business. Many successful entrepreneurs attribute their success to their recognition of a genuine market need (often a need unrecognised at the time, not only by competitive suppliers but also by the potential customers) and the determined harnessing of their strengths in the exploiting of the market opportunity. The aim of a professional marketer's strategy is the same as the 'seat-of-the-pants' entrepreneur: to conceive, design, develop (or buy-in) and market a product range which :

- satisfies genuine customer needs
- exploits real business strengths

## 3.2 What is a Product?

A trite question? No. A product is **not** merely a configuration of components, material, mechanical and electronic, in accordance with an engineer's working drawings. It is **not** merely an article of clothing whose prime purpose is warmth and protection from the elements. It is **not** merely a concoction of chemicals designed to given off a sweet smelling aroma. Indeed, it may not even be tangible in any way. A customer may have no tangible evidence of having purchased a product after the transaction has been completed: it may be a service.

A product is not just a physical thing. **It is what someone buys to satisfy a felt need.** People do not, on the whole, buy on a mechanical level. All products (industrial as well as consumer) have symbolic and psychological dimensions to a greater or lesser degree. They must satisfy not only functional, technological and economic needs. They often have to satisfy aesthetic, emotional and psychological needs of the buyer. Were this not true we would all, presumably, tend to buy the same model of car, wear the same clothes and holiday in the same place — within the limits of our purchasing power!

You should attempt to define your products in terms of the **benefits** they offer to your customers; in terms not of what the product is but **what the product will do** for the customer. Remember Madame Tussaud's.

Customers buy benefits not product specification.

---

**ACTIVITY 11** Consider the products offered by your business organisation. Draw up a product specification sheet for one of these products from the company's point of view and from the customer's point of view. You should prepare a pro-forma as follows:

| Item | Product feature (i.e. what it is) | Product benefit (which means that . . .) |
|---|---|---|
| 1 | The mechanical parts are sealed within a plastic capsule. | They are protected from damage by water and dust. |
| 2 | The lubrication system is sealed in. | Lower lubrication and maintenance costs. |
| etc. | etc. | etc. |

| Item | Product feature (i.e. what it is) | Product benefit (which means that . . .) |
|---|---|---|

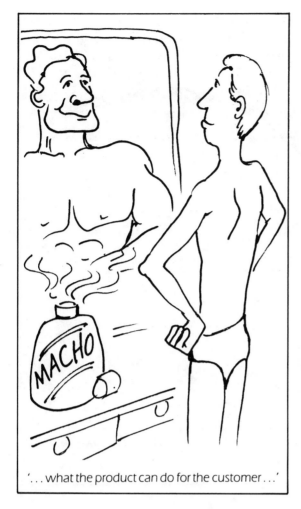

'. . . what the product can do for the customer . . .'

Discuss the product specification you drew up in Activity 11 with appropriate colleagues and assess how customer oriented you are in your product range strategy.

## 3.3 The Product Life Cycle

A professional marketer is aware of the constantly changing nature of the market place. Customer and consumer needs are always changing. So products will be expected to change to match these needs.

It is dangerous to expect a product to live forever. Many marketers find the **produce life cycle (PLC)** concept of value in their marketing planning. All products have a life cycle that parallels the human life cycle, and the cycle experienced by many products of nature (Fig. 10). Typically a product proceeds through four main phases:

* introduction/launch
* growth
* maturity
* decline

**ACTIVITY**
**12**

Identify and list the intangible factors that affect your customers' buying decisions. Discuss your opinions with colleagues who are not associated with your company, to obtain a more detached view.

The business characteristics of these phases are remarkably consistent across a wide range of product types (see Chapter 6, page 87, for a table on PLC characteristics).

In family life we normally expect the 'breadwinners' to be the adults within the age range 20–55 years. These are the people who provide for and support (financially and in other ways) both the younger and the older members of the family (indeed, in society at large, the 20–60 years group supports financially the younger and older groups). This is also true of product groups and ranges. Professor Peter Drucker has suggested that a professional marketer should analyse the product range in terms of:

tomorrow's breadwinners
today's breadwinners
yesterday's breadwinners.

It is important to be alert to the life cycle phases of your products and to be able to sense a change from one PLC phase to another.

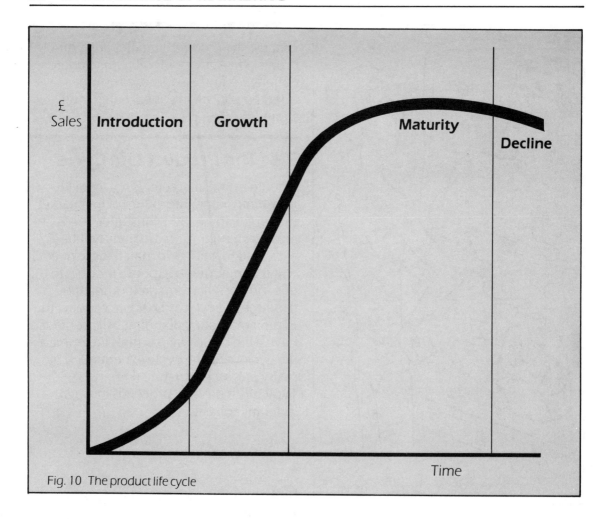

£
Sales | **Introduction** | **Growth** | **Maturity** | **Decline**

Time

Fig. 10   The product life cycle

**ACTIVITY**
**14**

a   Attempt to classify some of your main
products against the life cycle phases:
Launch
Growth
Maturity
Decline

b   Consider the practical implications of
this simple analysis for your overall
business performance.

a

b

## Product childhood

Once introduced or launched on to the market a product usually incurs substantial promotional and commissioning costs. If you have done your homework well the new product will have been designed to satisfy a known and well-defined market need. You should, therefore, expect a vigorous infant which grows from strength to strength rather rapidly.

This phase can be extremely demanding. It consumes huge quantities of resources and management time. Pre-planning for this growth is vitally important. Some companies have gone out of business because they made inadequate resource plans (e.g. providing enough working capital to finance growth) for this phase.

**ACTIVITY 15**

Ask yourself:

a 'Do any of these products owe more to the past than the future?' and

b 'Do any mature or declining products offer potential for rejuvenation through professional redesign?'

## Product maturity

At this stage growth in sales will have flattened out. Any further growth arises merely from an increase in total market rather than an increase in market share. The maturity phase can be extremely long. Indeed some of the best known branded products have been in existence for 30–50 years. Mature products are today's breadwinners. They must not be disparaged. The original investment may have been recovered many times by a mature product and the true economic value to the business is immense.

## Product old age

The change from maturity to old age is often imperceptible to the family but very clear to outsiders! This is often true also of products. Companies frequently cling to their past glories.

A sound product strategy leads to a situation where the financial burdens of the product range are borne by the mature products. Your financial objectives ought to be achievable without relying upon your old-age products. The aim should be to bring the youthful products to maturity as quickly as possible, and to retire off the declining products when they fail to contribute to profits.

## Product gestation

Before a product can be launched it must be conceived and then developed. There is no shortage of product ideas. The conception is easier than new product gestation and birth! Some people claim that only 20 per cent of new products (those actually reaching the market place) succeed.

During the pre-launch phase a new product costs — time, money, emotion, etc. — and earns nothing!

# CASE STUDY 6
# The Bradford Economic Development Unit

**3**

This is a striking example of the **packaging** of a vast range of strengths of a local geographical area into a marketable **product** (or is it a product range?). The strengths are as diverse as historical heritage, access to open countryside and the existence of a local authority team, elected members and officers, which is keen to support high technology industry. The mission of the Bradford Economic Development Unit is to stimulate new economic development within Bradford by helping existing Bradford businesses and by attracting new businesses to set up inside the local authority's boundaries.

The programme shows how Bradford set about marketing itself to the outside world. It had to improve its image. It had to raise its national profile. But it did not have the sheer weight of promotional resource available to the New Town Development Corporations. Every penny had to count.

Bradford as a tourist centre was conceived, packaged and launched; a hitherto unlikely product concept. It exploited the general attributes of the area, coupled with the weekend availability (contrasting with York) of good quality, value-for-money hotels. Sales exceeded expectations and the market is growing impressively. The benefits to Bradford of this entry into the tourist business are shown by increased economic activity generated by more than 30,000 new tourists a year. The main beneficiaries are the hotel, retail and other service industries.

But Bradford is also interested in selling other product features. Tourism is not a full substitute for manufacturing industry in employment terms. The **Bradford Marketing Strategy** recognised the **facts** that:

● new industries in the services and high technology sectors do not need to be located where the natural resources are

● the location of new factories is often more affected by the owners' and managers' attitudes to the local environment — its attractiveness as a place to live — than by the less personal, purely economic criteria

The creation of the new tourist products has stimulated more attention to the quality of recreational and environmental resources in Bradford. These can now be featured positively in the marketing of Bradford to business managers.

**ACTIVITY 16** If you are in the service industries ask yourself: 'What is it that the customer is really buying?' Is it:

the bald merchandise?
environment?
professional range selection?
merchandising expertise?
personal service?
impersonal fast service?
credit facilities?
image?
etc.

# CASE STUDY 7
# Ross Electronics

**3**

The company had grown dramatically over its first 10 years as suppliers of headphones, cassettes, leads etc. By late 1982 Ross were the largest distributors in the UK (50 per cent of market), supplying 66 per cent under their own name and 33 per cent under the large retail chains' own labels.

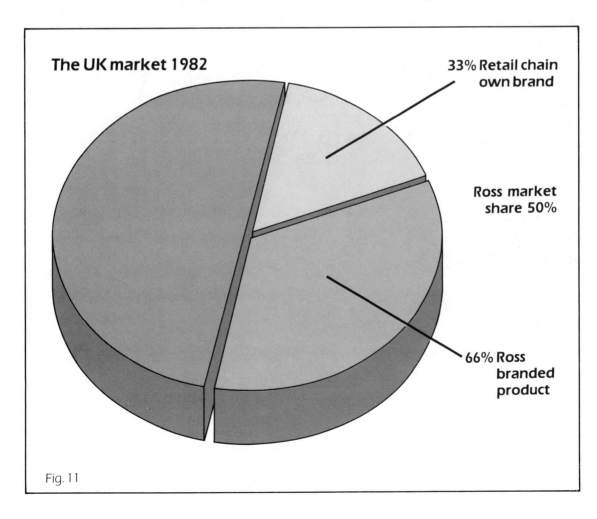

The UK market 1982

33% Retail chain own brand

Ross market share 50%

66% Ross branded product

Fig. 11

This is a very entrepreneurial company. The Managing Director, Ross Marks, spotted his consumer market for headphones. He judged the market to have potential growth. And he decided to exploit this market opportunity.

His marketing research activities included visits to Japan and the Far East, to identify suppliers and potential competitors. He designed the products for manufacture in the Far East, in some instances supplying the tooling to the manufacturers.

But the high street retail chains who became major customers still regarded the company as 'merely' importers. There was an upper limit to the purchases they would make with a single importer. This was a **threat** to the company's growth aspirations. The threat had to be accepted or be overcome. The company met the challenge and converted the threat into an **opportunity**.

The **strengths** of the company included:

- excellent **understanding of customer needs** — both consumers and retailers
- **excellent product knowledge,** including knowledge of what the competitors' Far Eastern suppliers could and could not deliver
- **UK market dominance** and understanding of the long-term market needs
- **willingness to invest** in the product range, taking a long-term view
- **willingness to accept** (indeed buy) **advice/expertise**

Armed with these strengths and facing the growth market opportunities Ross Marks sought the services of external design consultants. After interviewing a number, he selected Brand New who have worked with the company to develop an extremely successful Designer Range of headphones. 'The designers turned an idea into a reality', claims Ross Marks.

The industrial designers spent a couple of weeks in getting to know what the market needed and what it wanted. They examined carefully what the industry was currently offering to the customer. Armed with market knowledge and a brief to design a product range that was aesthetically pleasing (and very modern), functionally efficient and economic to manufacture the designers produced a number of concepts over a five to six week period.

The success of the new Designer Range is demonstrated in the marketplace. Not only has it allowed Ross to continue, as a British manufacturer, to grow in the home market; the company now exports to 26 countries and is proud to claim that it exports electronics products to the Far East!

# CASE STUDY 8
# Lune Metal Spinning Company

Lune was set up in the aluminium saucepan business, marketing under the 'Lancastrian' brand name. They have always had an innovative approach to business. They were the first to produce teak-handled saucepans and non-stick durable pans. These products were sold in the traditional consumer markets, although the company missed the opportunity to enter the mail order business.

## PRODUCT DECISIONS

Increasing **competition** and their limited resources as a small business led Lune to change strategey. In 1969 they switched to the industrial catering market. The size of the plant and the company's flexibility enabled to them to produce small batches of products in a wide range of sizes — **strengths** which could be matched well with the needs of industrial caterers. As the company targetted the industrial markets it also used its experience in satisfying the needs of retailers. They introduced consumer style packaging, labelling etc. to the industrial markets, thus becoming innovators in these markets.

Lune developed an excellent reputation in the industrial catering market for its range of pans, and carved out a major share. But there was an upper limit to the total market and to the share it could aspire to. The company therefore sought opportunities to **diversify** by exploiting its manufacturing strengths. The directors asked themselves . . .

'What markets are we in?' — Pans

'What business are we in?'

They concluded that they were not in pan manufacture and marketing. They were in aluminium spinning and forming.

'What markets might we be in in five years' time?'

Their search for new markets for existing technological and manufacturing techniques led the company to:

1 aluminium planters
2 crowd control equipment
3 the 'Grabbit' product

**Aluminium planters** were chosen as an important new product line following a modest market research exercise. The company believed that the US market for high quality aluminium planters would be significant. Initial research conducted for them by the British Overseas Trade Board indicated that there would be no US market. But the Sales Director visited the BOTB in New York personally — and found a large manufacturer of planters located in the same building! Lune appointed a suitable agent in Houston; now the second largest agent marketing planters in the United States.

## PROMOTION

Since starting the planter business in the US market Lune has opened up the UK market, which comprises plant rental companies, architects and other specifiers. They appointed a public relations company to reach these various markets rapidly and effectively. The architectural sector alone comprises some 4500 practitioners, of whom over 500 undertake a significant amount of interior design work.

The Lune management are strong believers in **personal contact** with customers. They use personal contact both to sell and to obtain market intelligence. They have used many exhibitions to achieve these dual aims: to sell and to obtain **low cost, effective market research**. For example, when considering entering the Swiss market for industrial catering equipment they exhibited in a Swiss catering exhibition. The exhibition stand cost them £1,500. This was a small price to pay for the information that convinced them not to commit more resources to this market. They discovered that the Swiss did not like aluminium pans. They preferred stainless steel. And they did not like the Lune handle design. 'Since the population of Switzerland is 3.4 million we forgot it. It wasn't worth it!'

## PRICING

Lune is at the top of the industrial pans market. At one time it shared the upper reaches with two other companies. But both of these have failed. They were not as effective at marketing as the Lune team. This left the company at the top. 'So we're the biggest, the Rolls-Royce. The top end of the market is the only place we can be.' The competition is always prepared to undercut Lune's prices. The company therefore has to cope with the problems of giving price leadership in this market. Consequently it emphasises both **quality and service** in its business proposition. 'If an hotelier or distributor needs a particular pan he needs it *now* — next week to get it cheaper is no good at all. We give that service. And our customers are happy to pay for it.'

**Pricing the planters** is a different problem. The company issues a published price list. For small quantities their prices are higher than their competitors. But they have a carefully constructed trade discount structure which reflects purchase quantities, customer requirements for service etc. The price structure aims to ensure that all types of customer are happy with their particular contracts.

> The last thing we want to talk about is price. The superior quality of our products demands a premium over fibreglass and other materials. We sell the technical features, the aesthetic qualities and the other benefits of the products. The price comes last.

However, the company does recognise that different market segments have different requirements and values, and may have different price sensitivites (see Chapter 6, page 83).

# CASE STUDY 9
# Tip Top

Tip Top is a retail chain of some 70 shops marketing toiletries and 'lifestyle' products (e.g. health foods, vitamin supplements, cosmetics, generic wholefoods, fruit juices etc).

Fig. 12

Having acquired the Discount for Beauty chain of 40 shops in 1982 the company recognised that it needed to take stock of its position and to alter its style. It had to be transformed from the family business style into a more formal modern operation. Improvments in organisation structure, top management capability and systems were to be accompanied by the modernisation of the company **image**. A **re-design** of the stores was necessary — and the creation of a new corporate identity.

Market research had shown that the name Tip Top was strong in the North. They did not seek change for the sake of change and therefore briefed Conran Associates, the industrial design consultants, to develop a new store design scheme retaining the name Tip Top. The designers' task was to create a new image for the company which was compatible with the range of merchandise on offer. A white, clean, zippy image was sought by the client. The interior design had to reconcile consumer needs with retailer needs. The designers were to create an environment in which it was comfortable and convenient to shop; an environment that inspired confidence in customers seeking to buy toiletries and lifestyle products. The final design created an environment in which the consumer is happy to linger while making her/his purchases.

*Fig. 13*

This retail organisation has recognised that consumers do not only buy the merchandise from the shelves. They also buy a mix of intangible product benefits which derive entirely from the retailer's function. Consumers have considerable choice of suppliers in the high street, in out-of-town stores, through direct selling channels etc. Tip Top's investment in the re-design of the stores, the re-birth of their corporate image is, in effect, the re-packaging of their retail services.

# CASE STUDY 10
# Cadbury's Wispa

Cadbury's developed this new product in conjunction with a new product development consultancy, Craton, Lodge & Knight. In the first instance the consultants were given a very broad brief: to produce a successful product using **aerated Cadbury's Dairy Milk**. This material, Cadbury's Dairy Milk (CDM) is an all-time great product, and there can be few people in Britain who have not tasted it.

### THE BRIEF

The consultants asked Cadbury's to broaden the brief, enabling the new product to be designed in a new shape if this were appropriate. After all, the Cadbury's Flake is just that — CDM material retextured and reshaped into a flake, indeed

Fig. 14

a new brand. The CDM material was analysed objectively and compared with cheese: a familiar material available in different manifestations. It can be shaped in many ways. It can be aerated with fine holes or with large Gruyere cheese-like holes. Many options were investigated and the research and development team were asked to produce different sizes and shapes. The creative people were commissioned to develop visual images which would help consumers to see what the product would be. Concept boards and mock-up advertising and packaging were produced for consumer evaluation. 'One of the difficulties at this stage,' says Creenagh Lodge, consultant, 'is that in the confectionery area people have very strong opinions but very low vocabulary. They're dying to tell you why they like or don't like a choccie bar. But actually they have no adequate vocabulary to do so.'

Having developed the mock-up product, and produced the concept board (which conveys the idea) the company was able to go out to the consumer, to explore and develop the idea.

## THE STREET FOOD IDEA

The new product concept was favourably received during the research phase. 'We also discovered that a lot of the classic offerings in chocolate, while absolutely delicious, are not adapted to what you might call the "street food idea",' says Creenagh Lodge.

'In some ways what we had discovered through this exercise of exploring texture was that we had developed a new kind of chocolate particularly adapted for today's out and about needs. And a great deal of confectionery is consumed in that way nowadays. Chocolate has become the fastest kind of fast food you can get hold of. If you're driving down the motorway and you're very hungry you may want to stop for a steak and a salad. Failing that you might settle for a pie, or a sandwich . . . or whatever is available. But what you can always get is chocolate confectionery.'

What Cadbury's have done is to identify this **market opportunity** for a street food convenience product. They have **matched this modern market** need by developing their well established CDM (beloved in terms of flavour and familiarity) in a **brand new** form, **shaped and packaged** appropriate for today.

## TEST MARKETING

Once the research had proved favourable the new product was handed to the advertising agency who had to plan a total promotion programme. The product was test marketing in one region — the Tyne/Tees commercial television region. A high investment was made in advertising and sales promotion and the product fulfilled its promise in the marketplace. Following this test marketing exercise the company scaled up to a national marketing operation, by which time Rowntree Mackintosh had introduced a similarly-shaped version of the well established Aero — the Rowntree aerated chocolate. Both products are now competing for the consumer's spend on 'streetfood'. It remains to be seen which company will finish the strongest.

Of key importance is the evolution of the **countline chocolate bar** — the chocolate product to be picked up and eaten as a single unit. Wispa has joined the growth of this product sector which reflects changes in modern lifestyles (see the Rowntree Mackintosh case study in Chapter 5).

 Chapter 5.1 to 5.5

# CHAPTER 4

# PLACE DECISIONS

## 4.1 The Importance of Place

It is no use devising (or buying in) good products — products which are designed to satisfy known market needs — unless these products are readily available to customers, in other words available in the **right places** at the **right time. Distribution** is an essential element of marketing planning and operations. It involves far more than the mere physical transportation of products. It is concerned with all **place** aspects of products and services. In some businesses the place decisions are of more relevance to the customers than any other Marketing Mix decisions. In some retail businesses there can be little doubt that store location is of paramount importance and that the level of promotional expenditure required to compensate for a poor location is prohibitive.

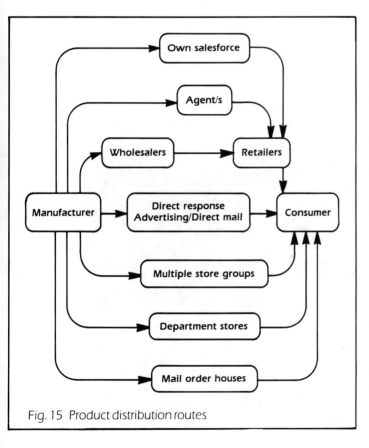

Fig. 15 Product distribution routes

## 4.2 The Strategic Issues

Products and services may be delivered direct to the ultimate users/consumers. Alternatively they may be distributed through a network of intermediaries, including such organisations as wholesalers, mail order houses, cash and carry companies, multiple retailers and department stores. They may use salaried (or commission-based) sales personnel or they may use self-employed agents to sell on their behalf. Figure 15 indicates a selection of possible routes for a garment manufacturer wishing to sell a range of ladies clothing.

All of these routes are possible. All exist, and all are used. Why is the variety necessary?

Each channel (or route) of distribution has its costs and its benefits. It is clear that every intermediary along the route will require a financial benefit. They will expect a **trade discount**, a **trade price**, a **commission** etc. This is reasonable and necessary. It does mean, of course, that the original producer of the product or service receives a price that is lower than that paid by the ultimate consumer. So why not miss out all of the **middle men**? The case studies included in **The Marketing Mix** TV programmes show many examples of the different company approaches to place decisions.

The key strategic distribution channel questions are:

1 What does it **cost** (from originator to consumer) to distribute our product through each route?
2 What are the **costs of each stage** in the route?
3 What are the **benefits** offered (to buyers and sellers) by each stage in the route?
4 Do 2 and 3 make **business sense**?
5 Even if it would be more profitable for us to **cut out some of the middle men** could we afford to do this?

ACTIVITY
17

What sort of distribution system does your organisation use? Assess the costs and benefits of the present channels.

For example, if the garment company wishes to sell direct to middle-class ladies via direct-response advertising it may choose (as some do) to use full-page advertisements in *The Sunday Times* colour supplement. One such insertion would cost around £16,000. How many would they need to achieve a profitable level of sales? How does the risk of a £16,000 media invoice for a one-off advertisement compare with the employment of a salesperson who would sell via intermediaries? Would the retailer's profit margin compensate for the risks of direct selling?

## 4.3  Distribution Added Value

Probably the most useful way of viewing the distribution channel questions is to ask to what extent each intermediary **adds value** to the intrinsic product. Each link in the distribution channel must add value to justify its costs. For instance, a wholesaler may add value because he provides a convenient one-stop buying location for small retailers. Your range is displayed alongside other products – both complementary and competitive. From his retail buyer's point of view he is providing a ready and convenient marketplace affording choice. From your point of view he is bringing potential customers to the place where your goods are on display. He is staffing the display, stocking and promoting it. And while he pays you less for the goods than the retailers might have paid you he is probably reaching traders you could not reach economically.

ACTIVITY
18

In some industries many wholesalers have gone out of business. The food industry is perhaps the most significant example. How much do you think this is related to the failure of the distribution system of which they are a part?

Small shops have suffered a colossal decline as the large-scale retailing revolution has been taking place over the past 20 years. One-stop shopping, bulk buying, heavy discounting, environmental improvements and new technology have taken their toll of the

Fig. 16  One-stop shopping – the wholesaler

smaller shops. As the giant multiples have grown they have developed enormous negotiating power as buyers and have bought from manufacturers in much bigger quantities than many wholesalers. Some fmcg wholesalers indeed sell some products to their retailers at prices that are the retail selling prices in large multiples. The really professional fmcg wholesalers have become aggressive marketers. They invest heavily in promotion. They develop very attractive trade Cash and Carry buildings. They stock highly saleable ranges. And they make extensive use of special promotional deals with manufacturers in order to achieve high purchasing volumes.

But those wholesalers who have not learnt to 'think marketing' have been, and are, going to the wall. They are no longer buying in bulk. They do not promote their ranges. They use cost-derived pricing. They fail to invest in their sales environment. In short, they fail to add value to the product as it proceeds towards the ultimate consumer.

## CASE STUDY 11
# Roy Hall Cash & Carry

In 1962, Roy Hall began to supply shops and schools with crisps and confectionery on a van-sales basis, from a garage at the back of a house in Manchester's Moss Side.

A year later he bought a sweet shop and converted it into a confectionery Cash & Carry.

Within twelve months the little shop was outgrown and a second move was made to an old Co-op supermarket.

Inspired by a visit to the Harrogate Toy Fair in 1965, Roy Hall diversified into toys and this saw a financial turning point for the business. From the success of this venture, coupled with the growing sales in confectionery and tobacco, came the impetus to build a brand-new 20000 sq. ft. warehouse at Ashton Old Road. The opening of this building in 1972 was a tremendous success, and from a turnover in 1963 of £350 per week, Roy Hall Cash & Carry achieved, by December 1984, an annual turnover in excess of £16 million.

### SUCCESS

The company's success is undoubtedly based on the effective teamwork of a management and staff who all believe in **putting their customers first** and providing them with **a comprehensive range of goods, competitive prices**, and **a high standard of personal service**, backed by the benefits of **a sophisticated computerised stock control and invoicing system**.

### INVESTMENT IN NEW WAREHOUSE

A further expansion occurred in summer 1985 when Roy Hall Cash & Carry moved to a new 60000 sq. ft. warehouse in Manchester — less than one mile from the previous premises, and three times bigger.

The £3.5 million investment required for such a development was very large for a family business but has been more than justified. It will secure the future of the company.

## COMPETITION

This case study demonstrates that a progressive marketing orientated management can achieve success in a highly competitive environment. The massive concentration of retail sales into fewer hands over recent years has resulted in the closure of many small shops and the failure of many wholesalers who have not moved with the times. Over 50 per cent of food sales in Britain go through a dozen multiple chains of stores, and two-thirds of all retail sales now go through these multiples.

Roy Hall Cash & Carry has prospered in this competitive environment by providing a valuable service — by 'adding value' to the products, so that . . .

- manufacturers benefit by selling in large quantities to Roy Hall
- retailers benefit because the expert buying enables Roy Hall to offer keen prices and many special promotions
- retailers benefit from purchasing a wide range of food, confectionery and drygoods under a single roof in a pleasant environment
- retailers benefit from the efficient computerised administrative system

# CASE STUDY 12
# Retailing

**7**

## STORE LOCATION

The massive trend towards the concentration of retailing into fewer, larger multiples has facilitated a trend towards much larger units relocated from the high street to the outskirts of towns. This has created much larger selling spaces combined with increased car parking.

Consumers are increasingly requiring one-stop stopping with convenient car parking. The big chains are complying. Even Marks and Spencer and Tesco have recently announced plans to develop jointly a number of superstore sites across the country.

## MERCHANDISE LOCATION WITHIN THE STORE

A manufacturer should seek to obtain an in-store location for the merchandise which affords the maximum exposure to customers. The favoured positions are often the eye-level shelves and the ends of the display gondolas. The role of merchandising is to site products in those areas which receive the greatest volume of customer traffic. The aim is to expose the customer to more merchandise.

## LARGE RETAILERS AND OWN LABEL

'Before the late 1970s large retailers tended to act as consumer warehouses', says David Stewart of Conran Design. 'They bought from manufacturers, the manufacturers did all of the promoting, sold it to the retailers and the consumers bought it. Now retailers have woken up and are very much looking to create their own image in the consumer's mind.'

Each element of the distribution network should be able to **add value** to the product as it progresses towards the consumer.

## SAINSBURY'S EXAMPLE

Sainsbury's have built a national reputation for quality and efficiency of operation. The company's advertising concentrates upon image projection — the image of the Sainsbury own-brand/s. The quality image of the Sainsbury product is intended to satisfy that sector which wishes to buy at low prices but with safety. The Sainsbury own label products will usually be priced lower than nationally branded lines. Sainsbury's own label customers will buy at lower than the Heinz prices only if they believe that the quality of the product is guaranteed.

# CASE STUDY 13
# Allinsons

In the 1980s there has been a massive trend towards health foods and yet a lot of health food is associated with the open-toed sandals brigade! How does Allinsons, a long-established firm of flour millers, and producers of a range of healthy foods, ensure that its products get to the right place in the retail sector?

Allinson has always been sold through a number of trade sectors including the health food trade and the grocery/C.T.N. sectors. The company has a history of distributing through the small health food trade outlets. Allinson is *not* a wholesaler. Allinson is owned by Booker Health Foods, which also owns Brewhurst — the country's largest health food wholesaler. An obvious distributor for Allinson. It has been a wholesaler for many years. But supermarkets have now entered the health food market and the company has had to change to a classic fmcg mode of behaviour. Allinsons has had to bring its marketing thinking into line with that of the multiple chains.

One of the important display aims of the company is to get their wholemeal flour located alongside the Homepride or McDougall flour. This is preferable to their product being located among fringe minority interest products. Research has shown that Allinsons flour does sell better when it is located amongst the standard flours rather than in the health food section. Allinson throughout 1985 and continued in 1986 is the brand leader in the wholemeal flour market. (Nielser M. R. audits).

The in-store location of products can be highly critical to the volume of sales. Physical positioning can influence the psychological positioning of the product.

# CASE STUDY 14
# British Rail — InterCity (I)

**8**

## THE CHALLENGE

'InterCity' is both a brand name and the title of a sector or division of the BR business. As a business, InterCity currently has a plan which aims to achieve a £110 million improvement in its financial position, by a combination of cost savings and revenue improvements. This is very considerable when related to the 1983 sales turnover of about £440 million. Very substantial progress has already been made towards the target.

## A COMPETITIVE ENVIRONMENT

The market for British Rail's products is extremely competitive. The wide ownership of private cars, the increasing competition from internal airlines and high quality long-distance coaches (freed in 1980 of licences restricting the routes they can serve) are all threats to InterCity. The coach sector is estimated to have acquired about £20 million per annum of InterCity's old sales turnover. The M25 orbital motorway around London has put the whole of the South East within easy reach of the radial motorways, further increasing the threat from road competitors.

## LOCATION OF INTERCITY STATIONS

One of BR's strongest selling points for InterCity is 'city-centre to city-centre' transport. But BR faces a new challenge as the inner cities decline and both residential and commercial premises are relocating into the suburbs.

Access to the rail network is a key issue and BR has chosen to work closely with the other modes of transport. The **parkway station** concept is a recognition of the need to locate some stations with large car parks, outside cities and adjacent to the new motorways. Bristol Parkway is the first and best example. It is well served by rail and road — the M5 is just north of the Parkway and access into the city is easy. There are plans to open a second, **Iver Parkway**, in 1988, situated on the Western Region main line and the M25 motorway close to the M4. Heathrow Airport would be very near, and passengers would transfer by high-quality coaches to the airport.

## PRODUCT AND PLACE

To British Rail 'place decisions' are the essence of their product. Customers buy BR services in order to go from the right place to the right place at the right time.

Chapter 6 contains a further development of the InterCity case study.

# CASE STUDY 15
# National Breakdown (I)

National Breakdown has been in business for 15 years. It is a youngster compared with the Automobile Association and the Royal Automobile Club. When the company started business it was to provide a vehicle recovery service. The AA and the RAC provided roadside assistance but if their patrols failed to repair the vehicle the membership fee only covered towing to the nearest garage — not recovery to home.

National Breakdown spotted the gap in the market and launched its service to take advantage of this **market opportunity**.

Initially the NB service was sold as a complementary service to the AA and RAC. 'If the AA and RAC could not sort out the roadside problem then call NB for the recovery service,' was the basic proposition.

## DISTRIBUTION

The company had to establish credibility at two levels: the consumer level and within the garage trade. The first priority was to achieve a national distribution network; to get suitable garages recruited as agents.

To achieve effective distribution NB created a pricing structure that pays the garages well for their services. NB provides a marketing service for these garages and removes the credit risk in working for unknown motorists.

Until enough garages had bought the concept it was difficult to sell to the consumer. The proposition to the consumer was attractive but the company was new in 1971. Its competitors had been around for eighty or so years.

(We will be looking at National Breakdown again in Chapter 5.)

---

# CASE STUDY 16
# British Wool Marketing Board (I)

The BWMB is an unusual organisation set up to sell fleece; to sell all the wool off the backs of British sheep. In order to market this industrial product effectively the Board looked forward to the end of the distribution chain and decided to concentrate on retailers at the top end of the market, such as Marks and Spencer, to use British Wool in making their products.

By doing this the BWMB set out to create a demand at the consumer end in order to pull a demand for its fibre through the whole chain of distribution.

(We will return to the BWMB Case Study in Chapter 5.)

# CASE STUDY 17
# Grattan — home shopping

Grattan is in the home shopping business — the business that is traditionally labelled mail order.

The mail order business took off in the mid-1950s. The catalogues issued by mail order houses became larger and more sophisticated in presentation. Manufacturers of well known brand names became willing to sell through catalogues and extensive advertising was used. The real growth of the business occurred in the 1960s.

## THE HOME SHOPPING PRODUCT

The strength of the mail order proposition in the 1960s was the opportunity for the consumer to buy conveniently — to select merchandise in the home environment, to receive goods on approval, to try them for size in the privacy of their home and to have no-fuss credit facilities. Credit terms were very important indeed.

## INCREASING COMPETITION

Towards the end of the 1970s the great credit advantage was declining for mail order companies. Credit was becoming easily available from the high street stores. Personal credit cards were also growing in significance. This trend has accelerated to the point where credit availability on the high street is now the norm, not the exception.

In the 1980s easy credit, one of the mail order industry's major customer benefits, has been eroded.

An additional problem to the industry is that the British high street retail scene has become much more exciting. A new emphasis upon shop design, on shopping environment, on exciting merchandising has developed. This excitement on the high street makes it difficult to compete through printed catalogues.

The response of Grattan to this challenge was to offer their catalogues to persons for their own use — rather than treating them as agents and expecting them to sell to, say, the 12–16 customers the typical agent of the 1960s achieved. A real effort to make the catalogues far more fashionable and exciting was also made. The new home shopping image has been introduced and the convenience of ordering has been improved by developing a telephone ordering system. The computer-based stock control system backed by extremely modern warehousing and despatch operations enables Grattan's customers to check by telephone the availability of a particular product and to receive it within a few days.

## MARKET RESEARCH

In the 1960s and 1970s mail order businesses regarded promotion as marketing. Grattan now uses the whole range of marketing tools. 'With the introduction of a very significant **high street threat** from the specialist retailers we had to go out and research what our customers wanted,' says David Jones, Managing Director of Grattan.

Grattan used a mix of **internal market research** resources and specialist consultants. Company people attended seminars with Grattan agents around the country. These seminars explored what the agents wanted the company to offer, and what they believed was wrong with the company.

The **independent external researchers** also interviewed both agents and people who had never purchased from a mail order business to check what had to be done to increase the number of customers.

## CUSTOMER DATABASE

‘I think the major difference between us and a high street retailer is that we know every one of our customers. We know every item that each customer buys. And we know what he/she would like to buy but couldn't because we were out of stock,’ says David Jones.

The company's computer files contain records of all customer transactions. In addition the computer holds a considerable quantity of census data which enables the company to analyse its customer profile into socio/economic data. They can identify, for instance . . .

● the type of house each customer lives in
● how many children they have
● how many people there are in the household, etc.

Grattan can, therefore, target precise market segments from its database.

## THE GRANDFATHER CLOCK EXAMPLE

One of the Grattan executives believed that it would be possible to sell a £1,000 grandfather clock by mail order. A very attractive special brochure was produced offering a limited edition of 250 of one style and 250 of another.

‘Using our ability to target precisely the types of customer likely to be able to buy these products we mailed about 30,000 people. We sold about 60 clocks from that mailing at £1,000 each. Taking the profile of those who bought these clocks we then mailed a lot more people of similar profile. We have now sold all the clocks we had available.’

This is an interesting example of how the home shopping company can use its existing customer database to target individual offers to specialised market segments.

 Chapter 8

# CHAPTER 5

# PROMOTION DECISIONS

The Manager of The Marketing Mix is responsible for spotting customer needs, matching these to corporate strengths (thereby producing a range of need-inspired products) and ensuring the setting up of an effective distribution system. However, unless the potential customers and consumers are informed of the existence and ready availability of these products they are unlikely to buy. And unless the potential customers become convinced of the value of these products (when compared with the value of competitors for their money!) all efforts in researching the market and in developing the products and the distribution system will be wasted. The perceived **needs** must now be converted into **wants** for your particular products.

Every provider of products and services — large and small, commercial and non-commercial — needs to take potential clients through four key communication phases. The promotion programme must . . .

| | | |
|---|---|---|
| attract | **A**ttention | of potential clients |
| arouse | **I**nterest | in the product |
| create a | **D**esire | for its benefits |
| prompt | **A**ction | (e.g. request for information or a 'buying decision') |

Who are your potential clients (customers and ultimate end users)? What is your product? How does your organisation respond to requests for its product?

**ACTIVITY 19**

The manager of the Marketing Mix

## 5.1 From Needs to Wants

The process of converting needs into wants for your organisation's products is the task of the **promotion** programme.

A **cost effective** promotional programme will typically include an optimum mix of promotional tools. The selection of these techniques, and their relative weighting, should **optimise on the four stage AIDA process**. For example, a small company wishing to promote a robotic arm to manufacturing industry might be well advised to use a mix of:

- advertising in technical/engineering journals
- direct mail advertising
- public relations
- exhibitions
- personal selling

How many of these tools can be afforded, and to what extent, will of course be determined by the promotional budget. They all have particular strengths. The possible number of combinations is enormous and professional advice in devising a promotion programme is highly desirable. In the above example the company might well:

- attract **attention** and arouse **interest** in its robotic arms by the careful use of advertising space in *The Engineer* and similar journals
- stimulate and reinforce **desire** for the product's benefits by editorial coverage such as: in-depth articles and press releases
- facilitate **action** (in the form of buying decisions) through personal contact with a company representative.

## 5.2 A Warning

Marketing is often viewed as being synonymous with promotion. It is often regarded with suspicion as a persuasive process geared to selling unwanted products to unwary customers. This is a serious misconception. **You are not expected to use promotional tools to create wants for products for which there is no need.** But having developed products that you believe will satisfy specific market needs, you must convince potential customers of **the benefits of your particular range** against the

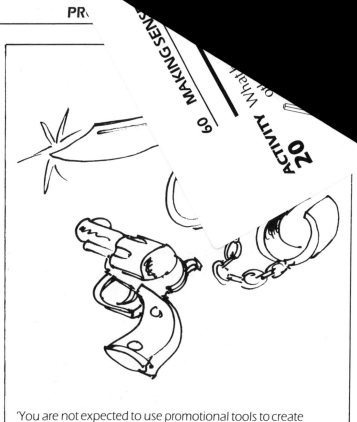

'You are not expected to use promotional tools to create wants for products for which there is no need.'

promotional efforts of your competitors (who may be in different supply sectors and supply totally different, but competitive, products).

## 5.3 Promoting Through Selling

What is the most powerful promotional tool?

Consider your own political views. If a politician were to stand a chance of changing your voting intentions how should he or she set about it? Should they use direct mail, public relations, advertising, television or personal contact. Most of us will readily acknowledge the superiority of personal selling as a persuasive technique. It affords the opportunity to tailor-make the promotional message to the receiver; to react to feedback, overcoming objections; and to prompt the buying decision.

Personal selling gives you:

- the flexibility to **investigate** client needs
- the flexibility to **explain** your product's benefits
- the flexibility to **negotiate** a sale

...benefits does your product give? In ...er words, what will it **do** for the customer?

**Good, effective selling starts with good listening — and with diagnosis.**
The qualitative advantages of personal selling heavily outweigh the other promotional tools in most markets. But the **cost of personal selling** can be prohibitive for many. A salesperson (other than typical retail sales staff) can often cost between £15–£30 per selling hour. The cost of a sales visit is often well in excess of £50. If you were to calculate the cost of an hour of effective selling time (i.e. the time a sales person is actually spending in presenting the product benefits) it would be very high in most businesses.

'Effective selling starts with good listening'

**Example:**

| A sales representative's costs | £ |
|---|---|
| salary, superannuation etc. . . . . . . . . . . . . | 12,000 |
| Car travel etc. . . . . . . . . . . . . . . . . . . . . | 6,000 |
| **Total costs** | **18,000** |
| number of working days p.a. . . . . . . . . . . . . | 240 |
| × Number of hours per day in front of customers or in telephone contact with them . . . . . . . . . . . . . . . . . . . . . . . . . . | 2 |
| **Total effective selling time** | **480**hours p.a. |

$$\therefore \textbf{Cost per hour of effective selling time} = \frac{£18,000}{480} = £37.50$$

## CASE STUDY 18
# British Wool Marketing Board (II)

**4**

The BWMB has an unusual task as a marketing organisation. Normally a company identifies markets and sets about arranging to buy products that will sell or to make marketable products. But the BWMB has a responsibility to buy all the wool that farmers sell in Britain. The BWMB must buy from four fleeces upwards — from whatever size of farm. The Board cannot influence either the type or quantity of material it must buy and sell. 'Our objective is to sell the wool as well as we can, to get the highest price possible for producers,' says Robert Wilson, the Director of BWMB. 'The sales turnover of BWMB and our subsidiaries is about £110 million per annum.'

### WHAT BUSINESS IS BWMB IN?

When the Board decided to become more professional and systematic in its marketing it aimed to influence demand. A prestige image was created and projected for *British* wool as distinct from wool in general. The Board exists to buy and sell fibre. To do this more effectively it defined its business in consumer terms. The Board decided that it was in the business of selling prestige clothing made from British wool. Says Robert Wilson:

> 'No-one buys clothing just to keep warm and therefore you have to create a desire to buy clothing. And a desire to buy more clothing. In order to create that you need something of interest, something behind it that will give an atmosphere.'

### SELLING THE ASSOCIATION NOT THE SPECIFICATION

So the BWMB started to 'sell the sizzle, not the sausage!' The Board recognised the natural sympathy of people living in cities for the idea of retiring to a croft in Scotland; and interest of city dwellers in rural society. And one of the most attractive animals to be found in the British countryside is the sheep. There are 40 breeds of sheep in the UK, all of them very different. Some have four horns; some are very pretty, like the Dorset Horn.

> 'We began to tell this sheep story. This jacket came from this sheep and this from that one. We've developed the sheep story very much into a British countryside story. A story of quietness, of lambs, behind distinctive products. And it was the way of telling this story within retail stores that attracted. It has attracted all over the world.'

### THE HERDWICK SHEEP EXAMPLE

This is a sheep with a fascinating tale to tell. It is now bred only in the English Lake District. The story is that the Herdwick sheep swam ashore from a wrecked ship of the Spanish Armada. It is unique in that the newly-born Herdwick lamb is born with black hair or wool. As it gets older its hair becomes light grey. It is a very coarse wool that traditionally went into carpets. It was not much appreciated.

So the BWMB invested this fibre with special dignity.

> 'What we did was to take the different colours, to sort them out by hand into different shades and natural colours, develop it into rather unique types of knitwear. This particular knitwear sells well, of course, in the Lake District — the concept of buying a piece of knitwear from a sheep you just walked amongst is obviously an attractive idea. As a result this product changed from being our cheapest wool to our most expensive.'

## A LONG-TERM STRATEGIC APPROACH

While the BWMB gets its actual income from selling a fibre it takes a long-term strategic view of its products and its markets. The ultimate consumer, the wearer of garments, keeps the Board in business. The intermediaries — the woollen industry, the garment industry and clothing retailers — will only buy fibre if consumers buy garments. They will only buy British wool if the consumer demands British wool. Recognising this fact the Board sells strategically. It targets the key retail store groups in the UK and overseas.

The first marketing priority of the Board has been to create products for its wool fibre — products that consumers could relate to, and products with a unique selling proposition.

Secondly, the Board works very closely with the retailers and major garment manufacturers; the people who make the basic decisions about what should be stocked. The retailers are the people who on the one hand put the product before the public and, most important, are the final trade buyers in the channel of distribution.

## SELLING BENEFITS

The BWMB has targetted carefully its various categories of customer:

- the ultimate consumer
- the retail buyers
- the garment industry
- wool fabric manufacturers

They have developed attractive consumer products for the others to manufacture and market. They have presented the benefits (emotional, psychological, intangible as well as technical) to the consumers through the retailers. And they have sold to the intermediaries the commercial benefits of marketing this distinctive range.

# CASE STUDY 19
# National Breakdown (II)

Having broken into the market for motor vehicle recovery by setting up a national distribution network (see page 55) National Breakdown proceeded to promote itself heavily.

## THE PRODUCT

The orignal NB proposition was to provide the recovery service that the two major motoring organisations were not offering. Once the company had become established, however, the AA set up its Relay system and the RAC its Recovery system. Both products were main line competitors to NB. The company responded by adding roadside service to its product range.

## PROMOTION

The company focuses upon four customer benefits:

- there is one office, one national control centre for the motorist to telephone for assistance (not a number of regional offices).
- NB's members can call the same emergency number 24 hours a day, 365 days a year and get an immediate answer.
- the phone is always manned by a trained engineer who will seek to diagnose the fault before sending the garage.
- because the car (rather than the driver) is covered by membership there is no need to inform the control office of the member's membership number; the car registration is adequate.

The promotion mix of NB includes **national press advertising, public relations, sponsorship of car rallies** (which yields significant amounts of press and TV coverage) and **personal selling**.

The whole of this promotion programme is carefully planned and the pay-offs from the various elements of the mix are monitored carefully.

The company believes that the most tangible evidence of the quality of its service is its Bradford headquarters. Big clients and journalists are invited as company guests to spend a weekend at a rally in Bradford. During the weekend they will be entertained in the headquarters and given a tour of the modern control room and offices.

## INDUSTRIAL CUSTOMERS

One of the conspicuous successes of the company has been its development of its industrial markets (i.e. selling to intermediaries who will sell on to the consumers). For example they have developed an 'own brand' product for the Caravan Club which the club sells to its members in its own name, very successfully.

Another example is the sale of the recovery product as added value benefits for car manufacturers. NB claims to cover more car manufacturers with this type of service than the AA and RAC combined. Their customers include Alfa Romeo, Honda, Toyota, Mazda and Mercedes Benz.

## PRICING

The price structure gives NB a competitive advantage over the motoring organisations.

---

## 5.4 Promoting Through the Media

In some businesses all marketing communications are undertaken through personal selling — and in some small companies this can make sense. But if you need to contact many potential customers this is very uneconomic. A company can make people aware of its existence and of its product range far more economically through non-personal communications techniques. For instance a 14 cm × 2 columns advertisement in the *Daily Telegraph* would cost around £1.10 per 1,000 readers in 1986. A half-page advertisement in a technical journal, with a carefully targetted specialist audience, typically costs around £20 per 1,000 readers. Compared with these, the cost of a salesperson's personal contact is enormous.

The **non-personal forms of promotion activity** may be classified under a number of headings, and there is a lack of consistency in definitions. A useful five-fold classification is:

- advertising
- public relations
- direct mail publicity
- exhibitions
- printed publicity materials

### Advertising

**Advertising** is the use of bought space, or time, in the printed or broadcast media. Advertising enjoys the advantages of reliable coverage, certainty and economy. Most media vehicles are well researched and have audited circulations. The circulation figures for many media frequently understate the actual readership figures. However, advertising is a one-way communication tool.

While the typical **cost per reader** is low, the minimum advertising investment to ensure impact in the target market sectors can sometimes be prohibitive, particularly in the context of the smaller

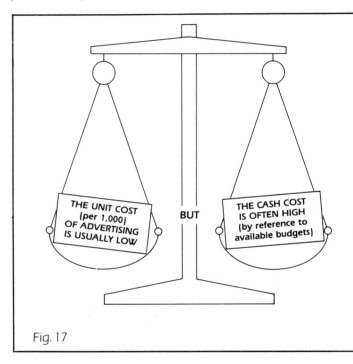

Fig. 17

business. If the **minimum advertising visibility threshold** (in terms of size and frequency of advertisements) cannot really be afforded, it is often better to conserve the marketing budget by re-allocating the advertising spend to other elements of the Marketing Mix such as public relations or direct mail.

The selection of advertising media to achieve the best result is a complicated business and cannot be adequately dealt with in this Workbook. Even within an advertising agency media selection is a

| Type of media (and names) | Circulation (1000s approx) | Approx cost (per sq col cm) £ | Cost of 14 cms × 2 columns | |
|---|---|---|---|---|
| | | | Price (Approx) £ | Cost per 1,000 £ |
| **National dailies** | | | | |
| Daily Telegraph | 1,261 | 49.50 | 1,386 | 1.09 |
| Guardian | 445 | 30.00 | 840 | 1.88 |
| **Regional newspapers** | | | | |
| Manchester Evening News | 306 | 15.00 | 420 | 1.37 |
| Liverpool Echo | 208 | 10.89 | 305 | 1.46 |
| Yorkshire Post | 87 | 6.13 | 172 | 1.98 |
| **Local weekies** | | | | |
| Ashton-under-Lyne Reporter | 52 | 3.50 | 98 | 1.88 |
| Ashton Advertiser (free) | 79 | 2.80 | 78 | 0.98 |
| **Specialist magazines** | | | | |
| Management Today | 67 | | 1,200 | 17.91 |
| Training and Development | 8 | | 170 | 21.25 |
| The Engineer | 40 | | 655 | 16.38 |

Fig. 18 The costs of print media advertising

job for a specialist — the Media Director. This is not just a number-juggling job. It requires decisions that are also qualitatively sound. An intimate knowledge of your customers and consumers will pay dividends in the formulation of your media plan.

## Public relations

**Public relations (PR)** is not normally concerned with a single public but with a number of **publics**. Some of these publics are of vital importance to the marketing operations, others are of more relevance to the financial and personnel management of the business. We will concentrate on PR for marketing.

### Press public relations

Public relations may be sub-classified into press and non-press relations. The aim of **press relations** activities is to obtain **editorial coverage** (printed or broadcast) of your activities, products, services, successes, resources and achievements. It requires the development of working and trusting relationships with the appropriate media — local, regional, national, specialist journals, radio and television. The job of the press relations officer or consultant is to ensure that the **most appropriate media** receive the **most appropriate marketing information** at the **best times**. For many stories the public relations officer or consultant will issue **press releases**, with appropriate photographs. For others, key journalists are invited to attend **press conferences** and write their own stories. There are other occasions when an in-depth article is offered to a single authoritative specialist journalist.

'An organisation must communicate with many publics'

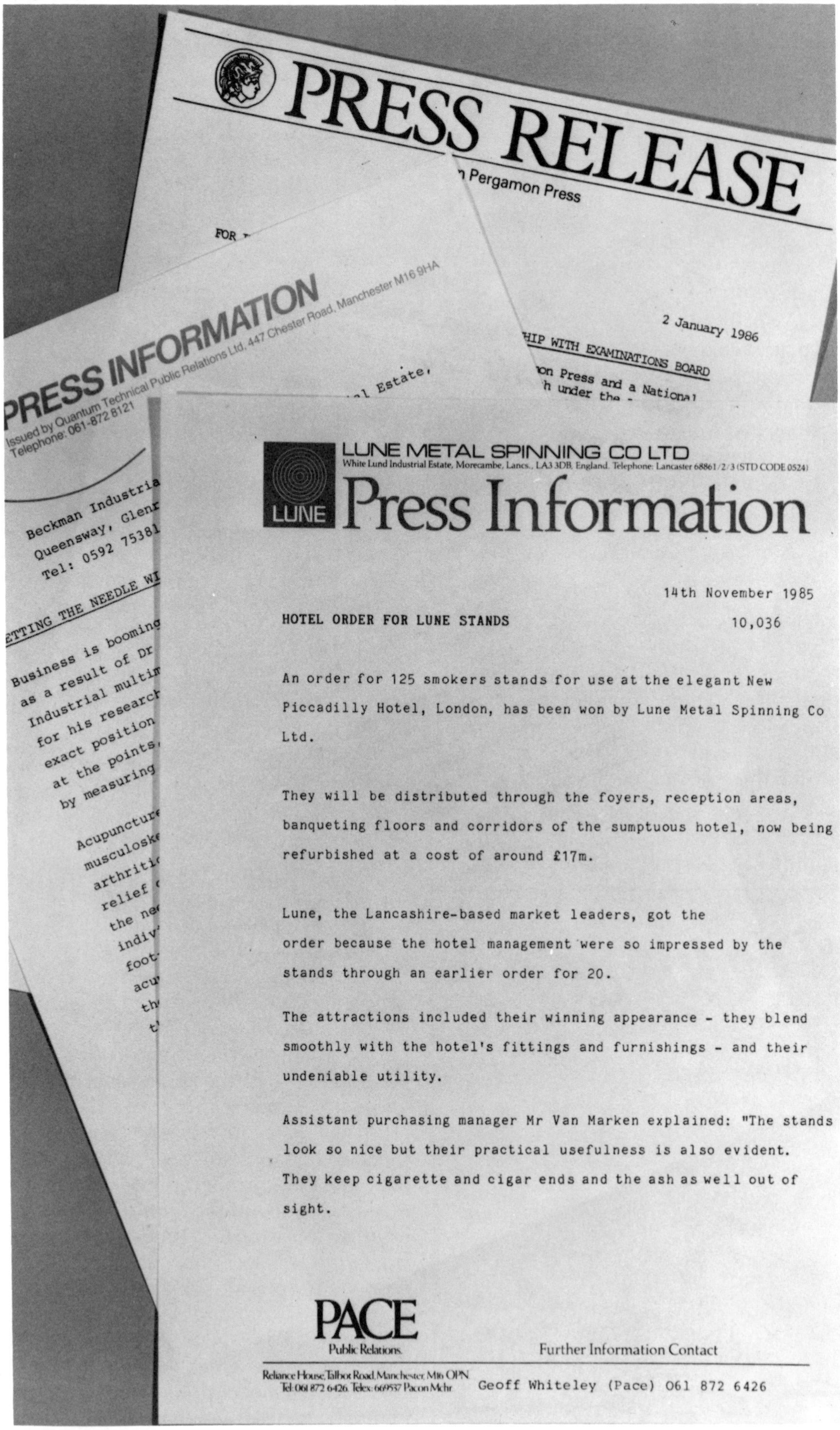

**PRESS RELEASE**

Pergamon Press

FOR

2 January 1986

HIP WITH EXAMINATIONS BOARD

on Press and a National
h under the

**PRESS INFORMATION**

Issued by Quantum Technical Public Relations Ltd, 447 Chester Road, Manchester M16 9HA
Telephone: 061-872 8121

Beckman Industria
Queensway, Glenr
Tel: 0592 75381

al Estate,

TTING THE NEEDLE WI

Business is booming
as a result of Dr
Industrial multin
for his research
exact position
at the points
by measuring

Acupunctur
musculoske
arthriti
relief
the ne
indiv
foot
acu
th
t

**LUNE METAL SPINNING CO LTD**
White Lund Industrial Estate, Morecambe, Lancs., LA3 3DB, England. Telephone: Lancaster 68861/2/3 (STD CODE 0524)

**Press Information**

14th November 1985

HOTEL ORDER FOR LUNE STANDS                     10,036

An order for 125 smokers stands for use at the elegant New
Piccadilly Hotel, London, has been won by Lune Metal Spinning Co
Ltd.

They will be distributed through the foyers, reception areas,
banqueting floors and corridors of the sumptuous hotel, now being
refurbished at a cost of around £17m.

Lune, the Lancashire-based market leaders, got the
order because the hotel management were so impressed by the
stands through an earlier order for 20.

The attractions included their winning appearance - they blend
smoothly with the hotel's fittings and furnishings - and their
undeniable utility.

Assistant purchasing manager Mr Van Marken explained: "The stands
look so nice but their practical usefulness is also evident.
They keep cigarette and cigar ends and the ash as well out of
sight.

**PACE**
Public Relations.

Reliance House, Talbot Road, Manchester, M16 OPN.
Tel 061 872 6426. Telex: 669517 Pacon Mchr

Further Information Contact

Geoff Whiteley (Pace) 061 872 6426

Fig. 19  Press releases

## Non-press public relations

This covers all other (non-advertising) promotional activities, including executive receptions, exhibitions, special events, lobbying etc. Many non-press PR activities are sufficiently important and large-scale in use that they merit stand-alone status. Indeed, there are specialist consultancies and contractors (for instance sponsorship consultants and exhibition contractors) who would not welcome their businesses being classified under the broad PR heading. The fact is that one of the key aims of open days, exhibitions, receptions and sponsored events is to achieve valuable editorial coverage; and they are usually most effective when integrated into a comprehensively planned programme of advertising, press relations, direct mail and personal selling.

## Cost and effectiveness

The **cost** and **effectiveness** of PR are impressive. Many people distinguish too simply between advertising and PR by saying, for instance, that:

> 'Advertising costs money but public relations is free!'

This is not true. It is, of course, true that the purchase of advertising space leads to an invoice. And no invoice will be sent for the printing of editorial stories and articles. However, PR must be worked at. A considerable amount of time is consumed in setting up and maintaining good public relationships. So PR should **not** be used 'because it is free' but because it is cost-effective. It is important to recognise that editorial stories are more convincing to the reader than advertisements. They may be compared with personal references: they can have more credibility than self-publicity.

This is another specialised business and many companies find it economical and effective to appoint an external firm of public relations consultants. (More information is available from the Public Relations Consultants Association, 10 Belgrave Square, London, SW1X 8PH: Tel. 01-245 6444/5).

Fig. 20 Logo of the PRCA

The power and cost effectiveness of professional public relations programmes is reflected in the growth of the PR industry over the past few years. In 1984 a research exercise conducted by Carl Byoir, a major international consultancy, surveyed the companies of the 'Times 1000' and 'Fortune 500'. The report indicated that the number of large companies employing PR consultancies had doubled in two years (Fig. 21). The UK was rapidly reaching the level of the USA in the use of external PR specialists (see: Anthony Thorncroft in *The Public Relations Yearbook 1986, PRCA).*

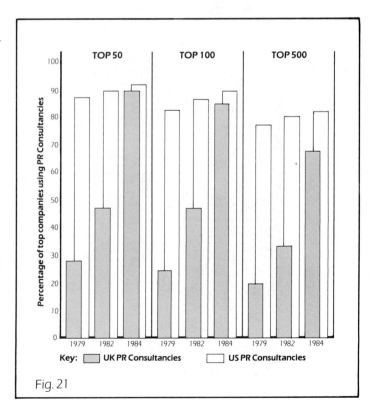

Fig. 21

## Public relations and the smaller business

While the statistics demonstrate the dramatic growth of PR in the large organisation sector you should not assume that PR is out of the reach of the smaller firm.

The **entry cost** into professional PR may be relatively modest. The managers of some small businesses develop competence in PR skills at a do-it-yourself level. Others employ external PR consultants to undertake specific (costed) communications projects. And an increasing number appoint PR consultancies on an annual fee basis. A small firm can employ a registered PR consultancy for as little as half the salary of a manager. PR is a very powerful, cost effective promotional tool of great value to businesses of all sizes.

## Direct mail publicity

Some businesses invest considerable sums in direct mail advertising. Because the scale of direct mail publicity can be tailored precisely to the available budget it is within the means of all businesses. Whether you are a national **mail order** (or 'home shopping') business, the AA or a small company selling house extensions, this advertising medium is available to you. **Direct mail** is a large industry in its own right. It is sufficiently important for the Post Office to offer advisory services to help firms to use it. Indeed, free postage is offered on large mailshots for first-time users.

To be effective a direct mail campaign must be professionally conceived and implemented. The design creativity of the printed materials is no less important in direct mail than in media advertising. Consider the sophistication and cost of the mailings you receive from the heaviest of direct mail users such as *Reader's Digest*, AA, *Which?* and the mail order houses. These businesses are very commercial, and they only use direct mail because it works for them. They are all creative in their use of the medium.

A direct mail campaign can be precisely targetted to specific audiences.

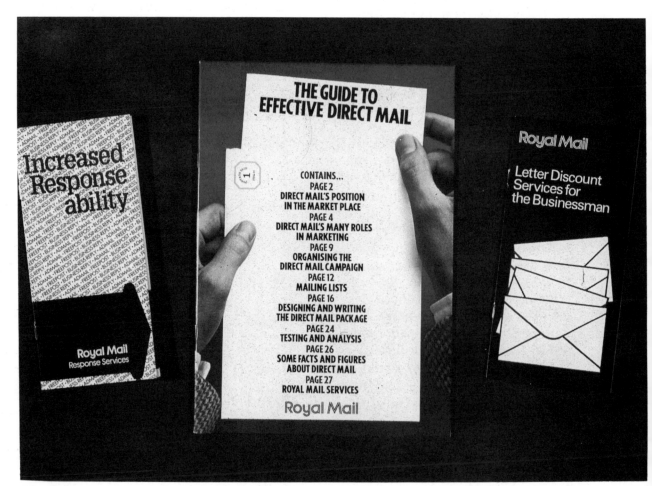

Fig. 22

'A direct mail campaign can be precisely targetted . . .'

'. . . an opportunity to combine the strengths of personal selling with non-personal communication activities . . .'

Wastage can be minimised and the unit cost of effective communications reduced. Success in the use of direct mail depends upon the combination of selective and accurate lists with creative publicity materials.

### Exhibitions

We have already recognised that personal selling is the most effective form of promotion, but that it is also the most costly medium. The cost of selling is the cost of time; time taken in setting up appointments, travel and waiting for sales meetings — as well as the effective selling time (in contact with the customer).

An exhibition is an opportunity to combine the strengths of personal selling with non-personal communication activities. An effective exhibition serves to bring many potential customers, at their expense, to a location that suits you. Many of the selling time costs are avoided and you are in a position to create an atmosphere on your exhibition stand conducive to selling your products/services.

A nationally organised trade exhibition such as the Toy Fair is a marketplace — a place where potential buyers and sellers meet. It is also a place where competitors can view each other's offerings. And it is a place where exhibitors are often approached by sellers. (Dr Rubic offered Invicta Plastics, manufacturers of Mastermind, the Rubic Cube at the Toy Fair. Unfortunately Invicta did not buy on this occasion!).

Exhibitions provide unique promotional opportunities, and are often focal points for promotional campaigns. The ultimate aim of an exhibition is to help increase sales. However, in some businesses the principal role of a national exhibition is to create and maintain awareness of the business. The task of generating sales becomes the responsibility of sales staff who follow-up visitors to the exhibition within a couple of weeks of the event.

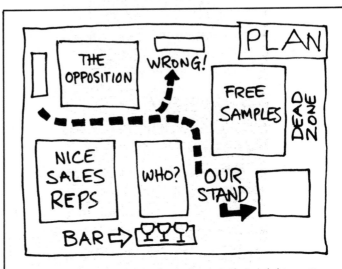

'Exhibitions are more complicated events than might meet the eye'

Again, exhibitions are more complicated events than might meet the eye. Managers who have not been involved in exhibiting before frequently grossly underestimate the total costs of the exhibition. The space rent is often the smallest cost element in an exhibition budget. The full costs include:

- pre-exhibition publicity
- exhibition personnel costs (such as salaries, travel, accommodation and subsistence, and follow-up time
- stand hire
- stand electrics and other services
- purchase of stand design, display boards, equipment etc.
- artwork
- sales literature
- public relations support

### Printed publicity materals

The basic AIDA principles apply as much to the development of printed publicity materials as to the other communication tools. In producing publicity materials of all types you should be guided by the following main criteria:

- the **target audience**
- the **needs** of the target audience
- the **benefits** your products offer to satisfy those needs
- the **existing image** of your business
- your **desired image**
- the possible **roles of printed materials** in changing the image
- the **relative costs** (including consideration of the materials, shelf-life and flexibility)

## 5.5  Back to AIDA

AIDA relates to all aspects of promotional activity. It can assist in:

- formulating the overall **promotion plan**
- designing an **individual advertisement**
- devising **printed publicity materials**

The total promotional plan must achieve the whole of the AIDA objectives. Sometimes an individual element, an advertisement, can achieve all four AIDA aims. But in practice a business normally needs a mix of promotional elements to achieve its objectives. In some instances companies lay particular stress on the importance of developing a **corporate identity** (see TV Programme 6). This overall, umbrella image is distinctive and impinges on all aspects of the business personality — from the AA's little yellow van to the projection of its distinctive logo on a vast range of publications.

Fig. 23  A distinctive corporate identity

In other instances companies invest substantial funds in the development of **brands** — distinctive personalities for particular products or product groups. Some companies who invest heavily in **branding** deliberately choose not to develop a corporate identity. Indeed they are often happy to see their strong brands competing agressively with each other in the marketplace. While **trade customers** (wholesalers and retailers) are fully aware of the company identity the consumer is usually oblivious to it. TV Programme 9 focuses upon branding.

Fig. 24 Strong brand images

**ACTIVITY 21** You are a marketing manager working for British Rail. You are required to draft a few ideas on how to reach the potential customers in the InterCity business travel segment.

When you have done this refer to the section headed 'Promotion decisions' in the British Rail case study on page 89.

## CASE STUDY 20

# The CAP Group (II)

**4**

The background to this case study is presented in Case Study 5 in Chapter 2.

## PUBLIC RELATIONS

The CAP communications Land Rover (partially financed by the Department of Trade and Industry) was used in real-life demonstrations overseas. It was taken to Swaziland in Southern Africa and demonstrated to various government departments.

It was shown how the Land Rover could be used to gather **agricultural information**. The vehicle toured the countryside, visiting homesteads and recording information on the population, crops, cattle rearing etc. This was new information for government administrators.

Its potential for use in **medical applications** was demonstrated dramatically. It was shown that a remote hospital could obtain medical advice from anywhere in the world through a simple telephone call via satellite. This would have filled a very real void in Swaziland, where medical journals are in short supply and usually very late. Diagnostic assistance could also be obtained. This was demonstrated live by making contact between a specialist consultant in London and the Land Rover in Swaziland.

This is an example of non-press public relations combined with personal selling techniques.

## CASE STUDY 21

# Heuga carpet tiles

**4**

Heuga are the market leaders in industrial carpet tiles; tiles which are designed for use in commercial and office environments. The customers of Heuga are industrial users, commercial users, architects, designers and specifiers.

## THE PRODUCT

The company offers flexible solutions to flooring problems. For the past ten years extensive use has been made of carpeting in commercial buildings. Prior to that the norm was smooth vinyl, compound or timber floors. This meant that office floors were cold and expensive to heat.

Heuga carpet tiles provide a more attractive and warmer environment. There is less heat loss and they are easier to fit than broadloom carpet, involving much less waste. They are easy to purchase (delivery throughout the UK within 48 hours) and easy to maintain.

## AFTER SALES SERVICE

Service inspectors are sent to visit Heuga customers some 6–12 months after the tiles have been fitted. This is to ensure client satisfaction and to solve any problems that might have occurred.

## MARKET NICHING

The company researches its markets carefully and identifies useful market niches which it can attempt to dominate.

An example is the **car showroom**. Research showed that while designers wished to use carpet they did not specify conventional carpet because the tyres would disturb or distress it. By using very solid Heuga carpet tiles the problem was solved. As an added attraction, the facility to incorporate customer logos into the tiles was developed using a laser process.

The **electronic office** is another market niche that Heuga has tackled successfully. When computer manufacturers were consulted, a major problem was identified; that static electricity can kill microchips dead! Heuga's first response was to introduce a wire into the tiles that helped to dissipate the static electicity. Nowadays they use more sophisticated treatments to achieve this same end. Heuga therefore offers in this specialised market segment assurance and protection from damage to computers and electronic equipment.

## PROMOTION

Heuga's promotional programme starts with research into customer needs. Having defined the needs carefully the products are developed or refined to satisfy the need. The customer benefits have therefore been engineered into the product and these benefits are sold to the carefully targetted market segments as solutions to their problems.

# CASE STUDY 22

# Heinz

'Beanz meanz Heinz' is one of the most memorable advertising slogans in Britain. Why have beans become almost synonymous with marketing? Beans have been a part of the British staple diet for a very long time. They have been around in Britain since the end of the nineteenth century, and Heinz started advertising them in 1905. There are few products which have been advertised so consistently in Britain for over eighty years. 94 per cent of all British households buy Heinz beans within a twelve-month period. This is a mass market and Heinz have carved out for themselves a 40 per cent share of that market.

## PRODUCT DECISIONS

A sound, marketing orientated company puts the highest priority on identifying a genuine market need and matching its own resources to the satisfaction of that need. Evidence of this matching is seen in the product strategy and the product range.

Central to the Heinz marketing policy is its commitment to the continuous development of high quality, distinctive products.

The importance to the company of its product decisions is demonstrated by the fact that every Friday morning the Board of Directors of Heinz gathers in the tasting rooms at the Head Office to taste 20 to 30 products. This tasting includes not just Heinz products but also those of competitors. The purpose is to keep the top managers of the business in close touch with the market; with how their products compare with the competitors. 'It gives us a hands-on feel of where our philosophy of quality within the company actually manifests itself in the marketplace', says Matt McBride, the Marketing Director. 'We pick up areas of discontent. We spot where there's a danger of losing a competitive edge. And we get reassurance that we have maintained the quality differentials against the competition.'

The Heinz product range is not a range of 'commodity' items. In effect the company is marketing **unique recipes inside distinctive packages (usually cans)**. Heinz aims firstly to produce a better product; a product differentiated from those of their competitors. 'Our beans have a unique taste. They taste different from everyone else's. We believe they taste better than our competitors', says McBride. And the Heinz market share seems to confirm that consumers agree with the company.

## THE IMPORTANCE OF THE 'BRAND'

Over the past decade the marketing of fast moving consumer goods has become tougher as major retailing chains have developed their own private labels products under 'own labels' or 'own brands'. Manufacturers like Heinz often feel disadvantaged commercially because they do not have the direct contact with the consumer enjoyed by the retailer. 'We have to find a way to contact our consumer without the ability to make contact at close quarters', says McBride.

The Heinz commitment to high quality must have a value in the marketplace. The company aims to ensure that any product bearing the **Heinz brand name** will have a consistently high quality standard from the first to the thousandth tin. The name Heinz gives quality assurance to wholesale, retail and consumer customers. 'Heinz is the brand. The brand adds value to our product proposition', stresses Matt McBride. 'You may produce the best bean in the world but the consumer may have a tough time believing that she should buy it if you have an unknown brand name — because that brand name has no credentials. What a brand name does is build up over time a relationship of trust with a consumer; a relationship which gives her an image and a favourable disposition towards the product.'

So the product is beans. The brand is Heinz. Put them together as Heinz Beans and you have a valuable product proposition — a branded product proposition that means something to the consumer.

## PLACE DECISIONS

We have already noted the strength of the competition in the retail store. Heinz products must compete not just with other manufacturers' products but also with their retail customers' own brands. **Selling to the retail outlets** is a vital task facing the Heinz marketing management. But **selling through these outlets** is just as vital. Unless the Heinz products move off the shelves into consumers' baskets the company will not continue to resell. The company must, therefore, compete for the consumers' attention at the point of sale. The Heinz brand must project itself off the shelf. The consumer must be able to make a visual connection between the brand image and the physical package. The Heinz beans packaging has remained similar over eighty years. The company is careful not to interfere with a winning formula. Although packaged in blue, now generally regarded as an unfavourable colour for the sale of food, to alter the packaging design or colour for the sake of a change would be to put at risk the consumer's ability to recognise the Heinz product amid the competitive lines on the retail shelves.

## PROMOTION DECISIONS

It is clear from everything we have said so far that Heinz is committed to major expenditure on its promotional activity. Having developed high quality products and packaged them in a distinctive way the company must invest in its communications with its customers — at all levels. The company uses a mix of all the promotional tools:

- Advertising: press, women's magazines, specialist publications and trade journals
- Public relations
- Below-the-line promotions
- Television advertising.

The various elements of the Promotion Mix are used for their particular strengths. Matt McBride again: 'We tend to use press to tell and television to sell — depending on the story we are trying to home in on at any point in time. We use the media which we think is most appropriate.' Heinz was, in fact, one of the first organisations to use commercial television in a sizeable way. Their early experience clearly paid off.

In the product decisions section above we noted the commitment of the Board to keep in close touch with the products. The management are as committed to spotting opportunities and threats to improve the effectiveness of their promotional programme. An example of how this works occurred when the *F Plan Diet* book was published. This best selling book highlighted the importance of high fibre diets for healthy eating. Within a high fibre diet beans can deliver the highest proportionate measure of fibre per regular serving.

The *F Plan Diet* book benefitted beans sales as a whole. Heinz benefitted particularly, though, because for about six months prior to publication of the book the company had been investigating the very same line of enquiry with a view to including the high fibre benefits in the advertising programme. Because **Heinz had been pro-active**, searching for new promotional opportunities, they were ready to take advantage of the unexpected publicity opportunity presented by the book.

## PRICING DECISIONS

Faced with retailers' own brand competition, a food market that is stable in terms of total market demand, the concentration of food retailing into fewer retail chains (over 50 per cent of food sold in the United Kingdom is sold through only a dozen retail organisations), Heinz could be tempted to compete through price, and sell on a discounted basis.

'Why don't we discount? Because we believe that we produce a premium product and we believe that the values we have on the product are worth paying a premium for. If we discounted we'd be saying that this is a commodity product. We'd be positioning it to the consumer essentially as the same product as everyone else's can of baked beans — but it isn't. Heinz beans have an added value; and the consumer is prepared to pay for this value.'

## PROFIT FROM MARKETING

The fact is that Heinz are the market leaders. Evidence suggests that their particular Marketing Mix, their combination of emphasis upon Product, Place, Promotion and Price is a profitable combination. It is easy to sell something for nothing and to sell it once. Marketing at a profit in the fast moving consumer goods market demands professionalism of the highest order. The discriminating consumer will not purchase repeatedly week in, week out unless the perceived value of the product is realised as it is consumed.

# CASE STUDY 23
# Taylor Hitec

**5**

This small high technology company designs robotic systems. It is in the business of convincing a manufacturer that it has the answers to his next manufacturing problems. 'Many of the solutions to people's problems in advanced manufacturing start as figments of our imagination', says Phil Robson. 'We can't go to a company with a preconceived solution to his problem. Very often we're going in describing a problem he's got that he wasn't aware of — where his market's going to be in relation to manufacturing costs in five years, if he doesn't take advantage of certain changes in manufacturing technology.'

## THE PROMOTION PROBLEM

The company was very conscious of its need to raise its public profile, particularly in the large client sector.

'We knew that we had to raise our profile to the outside world, because we were the David selling to Goliaths — a small company in a very specialised field; and all our clients are large, multinationals or nationalised corporations.'

The company needed to attract the attention of the big customers. It had to develop a sound image. The high technology, high quality, innovative features of the business needed to be projected to its target audiences. The company sought to develop the confidence of potential clients, of professional engineers, technologists and scientists in the technical competence of the Taylor Hitec staff.

## PUBLIC RELATIONS

The prime tool chosen to solve this problem was public relations. The company appointed Triad, a small PR consultancy, to undertake a series of small PR projects on its behalf. The PR consultants spotted newsworthy stories that had been missed by the company. For example, Japanese visitors had been visiting their development facilities over a six-month period. This was an annoyance to the management. To the public relations consultant it was an opportunity to generate news and to enhance the company image.

A story was written, contacts were made and the company got national press and television coverage, and local television news coverage.

The company also uses in-depth articles placed in the technical press, accompanied by suitable photographs. These articles imbue the company with more authority in the eyes of the technical public. In order to increase the chances of success of each PR initiative, the company planned its promotion programme to mesh in with relevant national events such as exhibitions. Articles were targetted at exhibition edition journals and complementary advertisements were used on a modest budget.

'The overall objectives of using PR weren't to try and achieve immediate business', says Phil Robson, 'because it's normally a more complex build-up in terms of enhancing your image.'

However, feedback within 24 hours of the first television news story included an enquiry from British Aerospace to carry out some consultancy work into an advanced engineering discipline.

## COST EFFECTIVENESS

Taylor Hitec was working on an extremely tight budget when it began its PR programmes. Consequently it did not contract in the normal manner for a 12 month PR contract. Instead it contracted regularly for single discrete PR projects. This has proved to be cost effective because the company has remained with a single consultancy — much the same effect as an annual contract.

To be really effective it is important for the client and PR consultants to have an ongoing relationship in which the PR people become very familiar with client needs and problems. It is for this reason that retainer fees are the most common means of contracting PR services.

# CASE STUDY 24
# More O'Ferrall posters

5

This company sells outdoor advertising space nationally on site billboards, bus shelters, airports, round-the-world yachts etc.

## THE PRODUCT

The company is able to orchestrate and change major national advertising campaigns very quickly. They claim to be able to change 10,000 sites in three days. Prime sites are extremely valuable and can cost some £100,000–£140,000 per annum in London.

A specialist division, Adshel, came into existence in 1969. It provides advertising space and services in bus shelters. This service can be carefully targetted. For instance, the computer database which catalogues the Adshel sites can be used to select 'all bus shelters less than 100 yards from any off-licence around the country — except Victoria wine', or 'any bus shelter within 100 yards of an infant school', etc.

The company recently ran a poster campaign, showing a small girl, called Amy, saying:

'Amy — I like slugs and snails'

on 3000 Adshel sites to prove the power of the medium. Research tests showed that after 14 days, 33 per cent of those questioned were aware of Amy and her message.

# CASE STUDY 25
# Rowntree Mackintosh

10

One of the largest confectionery groups in the United Kingdom, Rowntree Mackintosh are strongly committed to the promotion of their individual brand names rather than the company name. This is in contrast to Cadbury who focus the marketing of their chocolate products on the Cadbury brand.

## PRODUCTS

Many of the largest RM brands are many years old. Black Magic, Aero and Kit Kat are very old and still very successful. Aero is 50 years old and sells on its uniqueness, lightness and bubbles. Similarly Black Magic is very old. It is sold with a mix of mystery, romance and high quality attributes. The proposition remains constant but the presentation and appeal are constantly updated.

Aero, too, has undergone changes in response to the emergence of the chocolate countline bar as an important convenience food (see Case Study 10 in Chapter

3). If response to the threat from Cadbury's Wispa, RM adapted Aero into a countline bar

One of RM's most successful new products has been Yorkie. Launched nearly ten years ago with a deliverately strong masculine appeal the product was made chunky, and projected as being full of goodness — a very satisfying 'street food'.

## NEW PRODUCT RESEARCH

Yorkie was a response to market research which indicated a gap in the market for a really 'chunky' chocolate bar. RM's market research leads to the testing of new products — the number tested each year varies widely depending on the number of market gaps identified. Some products fail to get out of the test area. Others look good in test markets and then fail to sustain demand once they have been launched nationally.

'There are obvious limits to research', says Richard Gibb, Product Group Manager. 'When you are showing interviewees a brand new product you are showing them something they haven't actually experienced. They have never practised with it. So they can tell you, "Yes it's a nice product, I like it very much. I'm sure my children will like it. Yes I would buy it." . . . But what they can't tell you in any meaningful way is how much money they are prepared to pay for that product — and go on paying for it.'

An example of how new product research failed RM was the new jelly product, Junglies. It was a fun product which was carefully researched and well received. Once the product was launched it sold, but not in high enough volumes. It was too expensive for consumers to buy on a regular repeat business. RM are in mass markets and they require larger ongoing sales than those generated at Christmas and other special occasions.

## USING ADVERTISING AGENCIES

RM are major advertisers. They are so large that they use three regular advertising agencies concurrently. The creative ideas for their promotional programmes are all generated by these agencies. The company depends on them and demands good creative work. 'But the key problem is to ensure that the creative ideas are delivered to a disciplined brief — to communicate in creative and imaginative terms the particular idea about the product that we have determined from research and discussion', says Richard Gibb.

Each of the company's products is handled by a single agency. If RM are unhappy about the creative output of the agency they normally ask for a change of creative team rather than seek to change the agency. This enables the change to be made with the minimum of agency learning difficulties about RM and its markets.

# CASE STUDY 26
# General Motors

This American corporation is the largest manufacturing company in the world. Its operations in the U.K. include Vauxhall Cars, Lotus Group, Bedford Commercial Vehicles, AC Spark Plugs, Delco Electronics, Delco Products, Fisher Body, Saginaw Components, Electronic Data Systems, GM Hughes Electronics and GM Acceptance Corporation.

## CORPORATE IMAGE RESEARCH

In the United Kingdom the General Motors connection has not been actively promoted. A major research exercise has now been conducted to answer the question:

> 'Would it be a good thing for the General Motors operating companies in Britain if their ownership and connection with the American General Motors were more widely known, and given a higher profile?'

The starting point for the research was to identify the main types of 'public' that would be affected, i.e.

- people who might buy Vauxhall and Bedford vehicles
- opinion-forming or specialist publics e.g. trade unionists, councillors, MPs
- the Government and senior civil servants
- motoring and city journalists.

The researchers explored different categories of 'public'. The specialist publics were tackled by using **qualitative research techniques** (refer to Chapter 2). The general public were researched by using **quantitative research** techniques, in which 1500 people were asked precisely the same questions.

The research found widespread ignorance of General Motors but a generally favourable attitude to large American companies. They were seen as important providers of employment. Negative attitudes were investigated very carefully.

The general outcome of the research was the conclusion that a raising of the General Motors profile in connection with Vauxhall and Bedford would be likely to be beneficial, if handled carefully.

# CASE STUDY 27
# Halifax Building Society

In the mid-seventies marketing was to the Halifax Building Society a fancy word for selling and other promotion. Marketing today has revolutionised the Halifax. Taking on board the marketing concept has meant a reorganisation of its management structure.

Before the change the Society was organised along balance sheet lines, so that one general manager was responsible for lending and another for savings. 'We now see ourselves as a joint operation in the market', says Jim Birrell, General Manager, 'and all those services now come under marketing. They are geared towards market needs and what we can supply in market terms.'

## PRODUCTS

The Halifax Building Society now sells a range of products under the umbrella Halifax brand name. The Society now thinks in terms of packaging the products, promoting and branding them.

## PLACE

The Society is selling financing service products. It is in a highly competitive high street market and therefore pays considerable attention to the location, design and image of its retail outlets — its branches. Many of these outlets have been moved away from the commercial centres into the shopping centres. They have been brightened up and carry large amounts of point-of-sale display materials.

## CASE STUDY 28
# Lever Bros' Frish

Frish was launched as a new product in the early 1980s. A market gap was identified back in 1975. Lever Bros had identified a market for a lavatory cleaning product which was effective on the one hand and pleasant to use, giving a freshening smell, on the other. The existing products were either bleach or acid cleaners or cosmetic products. Consumers were frequently buying one of each type of product — one to kill germs, the other to freshen the lavatory.

## NEW PRODUCT RESEARCH

Working in conjunction with a brand development agency the company considered 26 different product concepts. They were narrowed down to three basic ideas. These were converted into mock-up press advertisements and tested on consumers. The consumers were asked whether the product would meet any of their needs. Considerable research was undertaken.

## TEST MARKET

The new product was developed and test marketed in the Midlands region. The aim of the test marketing was to explore the scale of the opportunity, whether people would actually buy and repeat purchase. The test marketing was very successful. There was an overwhelmingly favourable response. The information obtained in the test market was a remarkably accurate guide to what happened when the product was launched nationally. This test suggested that about 50 per cent of consumers would buy Frish repeatedly. This promise has been fulfilled. The nearest competitor has a 20 per cent share of the market.

## PROMOTION

Advertising was very important in the initial stages of launching this product. An educational job had to be done. Potential customers needed to know that Frish was a new way to clean; and that it was a new way of freshening up the toilet.

The key task was to get people to try the product. So small sample bottles were delivered door-to-door and distributed by Lever Bros in-store representatives working in retail outlets.

The initial, educational, phase involved heavy advertising. Since then the advertising budgets have become very modest for a fast moving consumer good.

Frish is a classic example of a new product launch. Although the product was developed to meet a genuine market need, it still required a heavy initial promotional investment, aimed at encouraging the consumer to experience the product for the first time.

# CASE STUDY 29
# JVC and VHS videos

At the end of the 1970s, when home video was starting, the two formats Beta and VHS were similar in quality and price. Beta was marketed by Sony and many people would have forcast that Sony would win the domestic video race. But they did not. JVC were the winners with the VHS format. How was this achieved?

## PRODUCT AND PLACE

JVC was an established hi-fi company. They approached Thorn/EMI about the possibility of adopting VHS for home video. Since Thorn/EMI controlled the largest share of the television rental market this was an important strategic move. JVC believed that the TV rental market was the key to video sales. The UK market for television was unique in that over 50 per cent was rental, of which Thorn represented a very large proportion indeed. To penetrate the home rental sector would be to dominate the system. And once a renter had bought a stock of VHS tapes he/she was unlikely to switch to a different format machine. **Distribution (through rental outlets) was the key.**

## PROMOTION

The company spends heavily on advertising in colour supplements, taking double-page spreads in order to be able to communicate a technical message effectively. They are also major users of sponsorships. Their sponsorship of Arsenal Football Club has put the JVC logo on to the television and daily newspapers week in week out since the company started to sponsor the club.

‘If people are familiar with your brandname when they walk into a shop the familiarity ensures that you go on to their shopping list.’

Chapter 7

# CHAPTER 6

# PRICING DECISIONS

## 6.1 Pricing and Costs

**Pricing**, the last of the 4 Ps, is a vital element of the Marketing Mix. Pricing should not be a cost-derived mechanical process. And prices should not be determined in isolation; independently of the other elements of the mix. The product, place, promotion and pricing strategies must be compatible and mutually supportive.

'Pricing should not be a cost-derived mechanical process'

In the long run, all costs must be recovered through prices. Cash can flow out of a business in many ways — payments for wages, salaries, materials, overheads, taxes etc. But cash can normally only flow in (other than as capital injections) through the prices it charges.

**costs** are a matter of **fact**
**but**
**prices** are a matter of **policy**

A marketing orientated business treats pricing as a key marketing decision area and not an accounting responsibility.

Despite this, research shows that the most commonly practised method of pricing is the **cost-plus** method. Using this approach a business:

- calculates the direct costs of the product
- estimates the indirect costs attributable to the product
- adds the direct and indirect costs
- add a standard margin to the total costs to calculate the price.

This approach to pricing will be disadvantageous in two main ways:

1 If the calculated price is above the price the market will bear (for the quantity you wish to sell) then the targetted sales will not be achieved.

2 If the calculated price happens to be below what customers would actually be prepared to pay you will sacrifice some profitability unnecessarily.

## 6.2 Differentiating the Product

Investment in product development, place decisions and promotional programmes may be aimed at differentiating the company's products from those of its competitors. The greater the differentiation of the company's products the more freedom the company has to establish its prices. Efforts to differentiate the products from others can influence the physical design and/or the image of the product in the market. In some industries the product's success will depend heavily upon the availability of the product — upon place decisions. The promotion programme will seek to add professional support to the other Ps. The image of the company/product will be very dependent upon the projection of a marketing personality on to the company's products.

When making a pricing decision a marketer needs to take account of the:

value of the product to the customer

price as an **indicator of quality**

**ability** of the customer **to pay**

**volume** of sales required by company

level of **market saturation** of the product

**competition,** in terms of their 4 Ps

---

**ACTIVITY 22** List some products produced by your company which you believe are price sensitive, then check this list with a colleague's opinions.

---

## 6.3 Customers' Sensitivity to Price

For many products customers are remarkably insensitive to prices. People like to buy distinguished (**differentiated**) products. And they are often prepared to pay for the differentiation (refer back to the section on the connoisseur consumer on p. 31). Numerous examples have been presented in the case studies that reflect an understanding of this aspect of buyer behaviour by marketing orientated companies.

An interesting model of value to the marketer who needs to price a product (which is based upon consumer research work undertaken in the University of Nottingham) is presented in Fig. 25 below.

Assume that the majority of potential buyers for a particular product is £1. The model suggests that if the price is increased there will be no noticeable change in the quantity demanded up to £1.20. At £1.20 enough people ask themselves the questions:

**'Is this product worth a higher price than its alternatives? Is it worth this price?'**
**. . . and answer negatively.**

Consequently, at £1.20 the demand begins to fall.

If the price were to be reduced below £1 the quantity demanded would often not change at first. Eventually a price would be reached — 80p — at which some people would buy more of the product, and some new buyers would purchase the product.

Reducing the price further to 70p will frequently raise the question:

**'Could this product be any good at such a low price? After all, you get what you pay for!'**

Many customers will be dubious about the quality of some low priced goods, and the demand below a certain price will therefore fall. To many people:

**price** is an **indicator of quality**

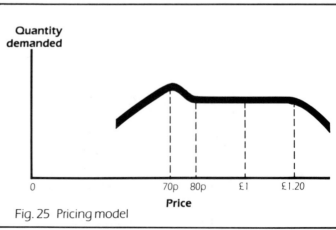

Cheap and nasty

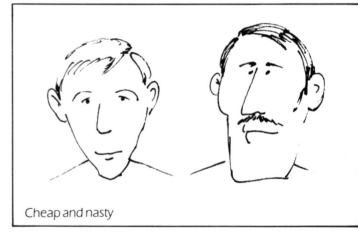

Fig. 25 Pricing model

If you are not convinced, consider the word 'cheap'. Surely it is a colloquial bedfellow of 'nasty'. If price were not an indicator of quality to many people the word 'cheap' would be redundant. It is not synonymous with inexpensive.

## A PRACTICAL EXAMPLE

We wish to buy a portable stereo radio cassette machine (a 'ghettoblaster'!). We expect to have to pay around £99 for a player of appropriate quality. On exploring the many retailers on the high street we are faced with a range of suitable alternatives within the price range £89–£109. A few models exist in the £80–£89 price range. Whilst these lower prices are very attractive we are a little dubious about their technical reliability, and worried about after sales service. Two products are available at £72 and £75 respectively. This is so much less expensive than our original expectation of £99 that we suspect very poor product quality. 'How could they make it for £72?' Since this purchase is for a Christmas present for a teenager we are very concerned that the product is up-to-date, of high quality and stylish. There are numerous alternative products available at a price ranging into the £200+ bracket. Having expected to spend around £100 we conclude that the stylish model priced at £109 will be a good buy. It will increase the chance of success as a surprise gift.

The Heinz case study in Chapter 5 is an excellent example of this type of marketing strategy. Heinz beans compete side by side with the own-label brands of the large retail chains. And yet they don't market through consumer price

discounts. 'We produce a premium product', says Matt McBride, Heinz Marketing Director, 'and we believe that the values we have on that product are worth paying a premium for'. The long-term investment of Heinz in the development of their main brand has enabled them to price towards the right of the pricing spectrum illustrated in the model.

Fig. 26

## 6.4 The Break-even Chart

In pricing a product a business must at least recover all of the **variable costs** of the products through its prices.

Variable costs are the costs that vary as the volume of sales varies. If sales increase, variable costs increase, and vice versa. The variable costs are those that are avoided if a product is not made and sold. In contrast **fixed costs** are those which, in the short-run (a period of time, typically around 1 year, during which the business capacity is relatively fixed) do not vary as the volume of business varies. If a product price is set above its variable costs the difference is known as the **contribution**.

## Example

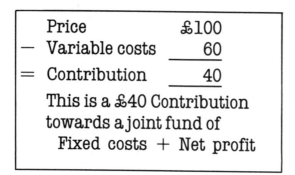

> Price                        £100
> — Variable costs          60
> = Contribution            40
>
> This is a £40 Contribution towards a joint fund of
> Fixed costs + Net profit

Assume that a small business has fixed costs of £1000 per week. It has a hole of £1000 per week to fill before it makes a profit (as shown in Fig. 27):

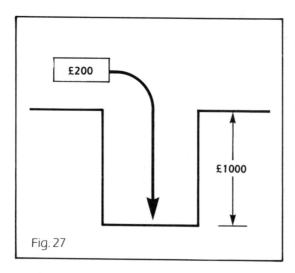

Fig. 27

If each typical contract produces £200 of contribution, five contracts will have to be sold before the fixed costs hole is filled. After that each additional slice of contribution adds to **net profit** (Fig. 28).

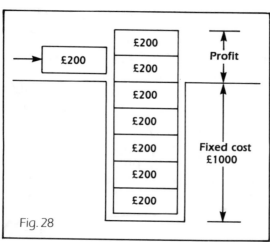

Fig. 28

The **break-even chart** is a simple model depicting the way in which costs and sales relate to volume of sales (see Fig. 29).

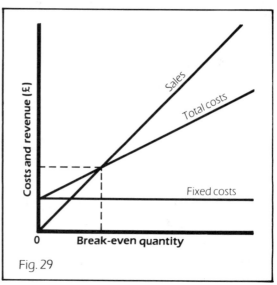

Fig. 29

The price determines the angle of the sales line (as shown in Figs 30 and 31).

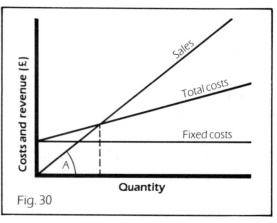

Fig. 30

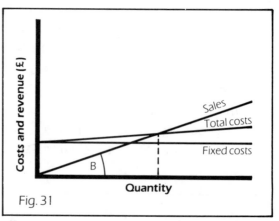

Fig. 31

In the above models angle A is greater than angle B (i.e. the price in Fig. 30 is higher than that in Fig. 31). Consequently a higher quantity has to be sold in Fig. 40 than in Fig. 30 to break even.

In organisations whose fixed costs are high relative to **total costs,** for example British Rail, the important role of the price setter is the generation of contribution. Every slice of contribution helps pay for the fixed costs. In the British Rail situation the variable cost of a passenger in the short run is perhaps merely the cost of issuing the ticket. The bulk of the operating costs are associated with tracking, signalling and the manning of stations; all inescapable in the short run.

Even their promotional cost is fixed in the short run. It does not vary with output.

## 6.5 Pricing and the Product Life Cycle

In Chapter 3 we introduced the product life cycle (PLC) concept. Each phase of a product's life cycle is characterised by a number of typical features, as shown in Fig. 32 below.

|  | PHASE | | | |
| --- | --- | --- | --- | --- |
| Feature | Launch/Intro | Growth | Maturity | Decline |
| **Market penetration** | Low | Rapidly increasing | Reaches its peak — often stable for long period | Decreasing |
| **Product differentiation** | Considerable. May be unique | Reducing | Low | Low |
| **Product proliferation** | Low (or none) | Beginning | At its peak | Decreasing |
| **Promotion expenditure** | High per unit of sales | High in absolute terms. Falling in unit costs | Stable. Often modest or even negligible | Defensive and volatile (easily wasted) |
| **Price character** | Relatively high | Differentiation amongst market segments | Levelling and stable. Structure established | Defensive and falling (relative to substitutes) |

Fig. 32

It often makes sense for a business to launch a product at a relatively high price, being ready to drop prices as the product becomes established and enters into the **growth phase**. In this phase it is often appropriate to segment the markets and to price in relation to these specific market segments.

# CASE STUDY 30
# British Rail — InterCity (II)

8

A business may sometimes sell the same product at different prices providing that the two markets cannot easily communicate with each other. In marketing a service it is sometimes difficult to distinguish between the corporate resources and the products. For example, is the Manchester to London InterCity Pullman service the product, or is a railway travel facility between Manchester and London the product? If the latter is the case, the pricing of products between the two cities is the same problem in each direction. But a customer group interested in travelling from Manchester to London has slightly different characteristics from the London to Manchester customers. A product is **what people buy to satisfy their needs**. A marketer should view the product through the customer's eyes. InterCity attempt to do this, and their pricing decisions reflect it. It is, in fact, more expensive to travel from London to Manchester than from Manchester to London!

A more subtle price discrimination problem for InterCity is **the second class business segment**. The success of the well established targetting of the first class business segment is revealed by sales of £70 million per annum in this sector. InterCity's market research has now revealed that the second class market for business travellers is already worth £100 million per annum to British Rail. (The economic recession has led many businesses and public sector employers to trade down to second class tickets). It is also known that many of these business travellers would appreciate some of the added value features of the first class product. Perhaps some type of intermediate product between first and second class will be devised. The danger is that these two market segments (first class business and second class business) enjoy perfect communication. Many members of one segment are indistinguishable from members of the other in all matters other than their willingness (or freedom within company rules) to pay the premium between first and second class fares.

While the introduction of an intermediate business product could earn higher sales revenue for InterCity it could also result in some business travellers trading down from first class and may significantly raise the operating cost of providing such accommodation.

## PRICE SENSITIVITY

The different market segments catered for by InterCity vary tremendously in their sensitivity to price. The bulk of British Rail's costs are fixed in the short-term. They do not vary significantly as the number of passengers varies. **Profitability is therefore heavily dependent upon throughput** — the number of passengers. Once the timetables have been published the tactical objective must be to fill the trains at prices the key market segments will bear. InterCity therefore identifies its periods of peak demand for business travellers (the people who will pay the highest fares). They then seek to attract the more price sensitive customers on to the trains during the off-peak hours by using discounting devices; in effect, by offering discount products. A ticket which permits travel on any train is undoubtedly a different product to one which is valid only on a restricted number of trains.

In May 1985 British Rail launched a brand new simplified pricing structure for return travel, based on distance and time of travel:-

|  | PEAK | OFF-PEAK |
|---|---|---|
| Short Distance | Standard Day Return | Cheap Day Return |
| Long Distance | Standard Return | Saver |

InterCity customers are therefore using Standard Return or Saver tickets.

In addition Railcards are available to carefully targetted market segments such as . . .

- the Family Railcard
- the Senior Citizen Railcard
- the Student Railcard.

'Backed up by the railcards that offer one-third off the standard tickets, one-third off the saver tickets and 50 per cent off the cheap day return we have a range of fares that is attractive to the market and at the same time reflects our cost structure', says Ivor Warburton, of British Rail. 'We retain complete flexibility within the price structure. We started selective pricing in 1968, and we've learnt a lot in the course of the years.'

Some critics of British Rail suggest that with much lower fares BR would attract a larger share of the travel market. But any fare change must yield a greater total sales revenue than before without increasing production costs. InterCity's research studies indicate that the extra customers that could be attracted at the lower prices if an across-the-board fare reduction were implemented would not yield enough extra revenue: the price reduction per passenger would not be compensated by the increased number of passengers. Hence the selective pricing and the importance to InterCity of **market segmentation**.

## PROMOTION DECISIONS

Few people who watch independent television can have missed the substantial promotional activities of InterCity. The InterCity advertising campaigns emphasise both the quality and qualities of the products. The campaigns are designed to add value to the InterCity brand; to create a favourable image. One of the advantages of such promotional activity is that it highlights the differences between the brand and the competition. Investment in image reduces the sensitivity of the customer to the price.

In addition to the corporate publicity umbrella, InterCity targets very specific market segments with its promotional effort. A notable example of this was the sponsorship of the National Squash Championships and a National Challenge. 7000 club players were attracted to the 1985 event. This promotion was targetted at the key members of the InterCity market for both business and leisure travel. Squash players have a high proportion of middle and upper middle class people in the under 34 years age group.

## PROFIT FROM MARKETING

British Rail depends heavily upon the commercial success of the InterCity sector. The board's 'InterCity into Profit' plan is essentially a marketing plan which is carefully conceived to ensure the long-term development of **high quality products** available in the **right place**, at the **right time**, and **promoted** in a manner that creates a **positive image** reflecting the quality and **value** of the products.

The compination of the four elements of the Marketing Mix, 'the 4Ps' is highly critical to the success of the business.

'Our product is quite different from a bar of chocolate', says Ivor Warburton. 'Our product is instantly perishable. We're making timetabling decisions up to twelve months in advance and we really can't easily alter the unit of production on a particular day. If a train leaves a station and there's a seat not filled there's nothing we can do about it. That unit of product is dead. It's perished.'

# CASE STUDY 31
# National Museum of Photography

8

This museum, located in Bradford, is a part of the National Science Museum. It pocesses an IMAX screen — one of only five of these extra-large cinema screens in the world, and the only one in the United Kingdom. Faced with the requirement to earn revenue it had a choice to make: to charge admission to all visitors or to give free admission and then charge for its special IMAX show. The decision was taken to give free admission and to charge visitors for watching the IMAX film.

It was considered that an admission charge would have to be modest, say 50 pence per person, whereas the IMAX show could command a higher price. The decision was taken to charge £1.50 to view the IMAX film. Some 38 per cent of visitors now buy this product.

## PRICING TO ACHIEVE NON-PROFIT AIMS

The National Museum of Photography does not exist as a profit-making organisation. One of its objectives, perhaps its main objective, is to attract as many visitors as possible. The pricing policy appears to have succeeded in achieving this while also earning income by exploiting the museum's 'unique selling proposition' — the IMAX film.

## CASE STUDY 32
# Yale Security Products

8

Yale is a long-established business in the traditional locks, handles and security fastenings markets. The company is committed to marketing as a way of business life. They take a long term view of their markets in an attempt to spot both opportunities and threats. New market opportunities are screened methodically against their company strengths, and evaluated for their likely viability. A favourable analysis of costs, investment implications and sales forecasts leads to a product development programme.

**Yaletronics** is an example of such a new product. It is an electronic security system designed to reduce the high level of theft from hotel bedrooms.

### THE NEED
In the life of an hotel room some 20–40 keys may be issued due to loss, non-return, theft etc . . . 'People just walk away with keys'.

### COMPANY STRENGTHS AND WEAKNESSES
Yale has had considerable experience of the lock markets in general and of the hotel market for locks. It has enjoyed an excellent reputation for product quality and reliability; for professional knowhow.

But Yale knew nothing of electronics. Because the market was large and valuable, and because the development of electronic locking systems by competitors would have been a threat, Yale recruited experienced electronics designers and engineers. Their expertise was combined with that of the company's own security experts in a programme of new product development.

### THE PRODUCT
Yaletronics is a system in which a central computer located at the front desk of the hotel controls all the bedroom keys.

Each bedroom lock is activated by a disposable, programmable plastic key. A new code is issued automatically and securely by the computer with each new key issue. The key may be destroyed on termination of residence.

### THE BENEFITS
Prior to the launch of the product the promise was that it would improve the security of an hotel. Once the product was launched this promise was fulfilled. A dramatic decrease in theft from hotel rooms follows installation. This is clearly a major benefit to hotel guests. It is also a major benefit to hoteliers. Beside the problems of dealing with the reporting and investigation of crimes, and the problems/costs associated with re-issue of traditional keys, an hotel with a Yaletronics installation could focus in its publicity on the advantages of its security system.

## SERVICE AND PLACE DECISIONS

To succeed in this market Yale needed to set up an excellent service network, which could respond quickly to problems. 'If you have a broken lock in the field it may take a month to fix — but in hotel security you could have 300 check-ins over one hour at tea-time. Fast service is essential'. Yale had researched its market and established its network of service engineers to meet the new market needs.

## LAUNCH

Although the market research had been positive, indicating a big market for systems of about £80,000 capital costs, it was difficult to get the first hotel contract. Yale targetted the London Tara Hotel and negotiated a **trial installation** on one floor only. It was successful and the whole hotel was converted.

In negotiating the trial the strength of **the Yale company image was critical**. The manager recognised that there might be teething problems. But because of his **confidence in the Yale name** he believed that the company would succeed in the commissioning stage of product development.

## PRICING

This new-technology based security system was costly to develop (some £3 to £4 million). A commercially acceptable price to Yale has to reflect both the development and the after-sales service costs. This pushes the price up to about twice the cost of fitting traditional locking equipment. Because of the cost of installing the front desk computer, Yaletronics is generally most attractive to hotels of 100+ rooms.

To sell, say, a £80,000 security installation to an hotel it is vital to sell the benefits

- to the hotelier
- to the consumer/visitor.

Yale have succeeded in doing this. Yaletronics is now the brand-leader in the UK. Success indeed for an old established company who conducted a SWOT analysis (Strengths, Weaknesses, Opportunities and Threats), researched their market, invested heavily in the development of the new product, designed it to meet the users' needs, backed it with an efficient after-sales service and priced it to reflect its benefits.

 Chapter 5.6 to 5.8

# CHAPTER 7

# OVER TO YOU

The Marketing Mix Open Learning package was devised to enable the viewer and reader to share the experience of other marketing practitioners. Hopefully it will have confirmed that your existing marketing operations are professional, and compare favourably with well-based practice. Maybe you will have gained insight that will inspire you to make improvements to your current marketing operations.

The case studies included in this Workbook are diverse. They include service and manufacturing companies, public and private sector businesses and large and small firms. If you are to get the maximum value from studying the material and watching the television programmes **you should not be content with simply acquiring new knowledge**. You need to examine this training material very carefully, asking yourself . . .

- 'Could this case have relevance to our situation?'
- 'How can we benefit from the experiences of Madame Tussaud's or Heinz — or Taylor Hitec . . .?'

In asking these and similar questions, you should put firmly on one side any preconceptions you might have about the size and nature of your business. The marketing principles introduced in this Workbook are applicable to all businesses. **The lessons learned by the large companies are often transferable to smaller businesses — and vice versa.** The challenge is yours.

Professional marketing is not a matter of applying formulae and calculating the solution to business problems. It is as vital for British Rail to understand the **needs and motivations** of its various customer groups as it is for the market trader. It is as important for the smaller company to create a **confidence building image** as it is for a large company to create a stylish **corporate identity**. Both large and small companies have to price their products and should be aware of the need to regard **pricing** as a central element of The Marketing Mix.

All of the case studies presented in the Workbook are examples of organisations committed to marketing as a philosophy of business; committed to putting the customer at the centre of their business plans: committed to getting their staff to 'Think Marketing'. We hope you will discover ideas in this Wookbook that are worth trying in your own situation.

 Chapter 9

NOW IT'S OVER TO YOU